HOW TO TALK TO
A YANKEE FAN

Andy Wasif
and Rick D'Elia

Hope this helps in dealings with Yankee fans.

SEVEN LOCKS PRESS

Santa Ana, California

Seven Locks Press
P.O. Box 25689
Santa Ana, CA 92799
(800) 354-5348

Individual Sales. This book is available through most bookstores or can be ordered directly from Seven Locks Press at the address above.

Quantity Sales. Special discounts are available on quantity purchases by corporations, associations, and others. For details, contact the "Special Sales Department" at the publisher's address above.

Printed in the United States of America

Library of Congress Cataloging-in-Publication Data
is available from the publisher
ISBN 1-931643-93-8

Illustrations by Rocco Urbisci
Page 55 illustration by Paul D'Angelo

www.howtotalktoayankeefan.com

DEDICATION

Andy dedicates this book to Victor J. Steele who never wanted pizza from Yankee fans, he only wanted respect.

Rick dedicates this book to his two greatest inspirations in the world—his grandmother, Eleanor "Na-nay" D'Elia, and his canine son, Truckee.

TABLE OF CONTENTS

FOREWORD

When asked to write the foreword for Rick D'Elia and Andy Wasif's soon to be bestseller *How to talk to a Yankee Fan*, I did not say, "Sure I'll do it!" I said, "You've got to be kidding! That book has got to be the second shortest book in recorded history, right behind that page-turner, *The Taliban I've Known While Yachting*."

Peter Gammons once called me a "Walking Non-Sequitor"—whatever that means. With that in mind, I decided that what I had been asked to do required some thought.

To start work on this foreword, we must define the word "talk." "Talk" is a four-letter word. Personally, I prefer the word "conversation;" it implies a two-way street. Now Manhattan does not have a lot of two-way streets and therein lays a fundamental problem. A mentor of mine, the late great Satchel Paige found himself, one time, with such a problem. He was late for a contest and on his way to the stadium when he was confronted with a one-way street. To save time, he proceeded up that one-way street. He was then pinched by a constable, who asked him if he was aware he was going down a one-way . . . to which Satchel said with all gravity, "That's okay, officer, I am only going one way!"

The English language can be very complicated. In Olde England during Willy Shakespeare's time, the word "conversation" was also known as an intercourse. Now, we all know what happened during Bill Clinton's presidency when he needed clarification on "What is . . . is?" (Do you want the cigar info?) So in 1918, when Harry Frazee "intercoursed" Boston and all Red Sox fans out of Babe Ruth and a host of other Red Sox players, pitchers, a catcher and a GM, quite frankly we felt all talked out. Coincidently, in 1923 when the Yankees won their first World Series, out of all the games played, eighty-one of the victories that year were by former Red Sox pitchers. All conversations since that time seem to have fallen on deaf ears.

Zip ahead to current times and that brings us to the minds and the anatomy of the Yankee fan. It is really amazing that they can wear glasses, or hats for that matter. I have always thought you required ears to support either. It is also amazing a Yankee fan doesn't die each and every day crashing into a telephone pole, because his hat fell over his eyes while driving. But then again, New Yorkers don't drive—they're all chauffeured around by Mets fans. When you start a conversation with a Yankee fan, you better bring a cork to stick in one of his ears; even then his thoughts will rattle around like refuse in a vacant lot.

Usually, when you talk to a Yankee fan, you don't get to talk first. That reminds me of a certain cab ride I took. In 1973, at the All Star game in Kansas City, I had missed the American League bus, so I jumped into a cab only to find Reggie Jackson jump in after me, and tell the cabbie "To the yard!" I tried to explain to Reggie that Kansas City was a cattle town and that we had better be more precise with the destination or we would end up at the feedlot and then the slaughterhouse. The park at that time was not Memorial Stadium, but Ewing Stadium: the house that Monsanto built. It was the first with Astroturf. That whole cab ride Reggie talked and talked and talked . . . he told me about his real estate ventures. He told me about his shoe contracts. He told me a great many things. Damn, I just knew he was a Yankee in training; I never got a word in edgewise. I learned a great deal about Reggie that day, he on the other hand learned little about me . . . in retrospect that's not such a bad thing.

Since that cab ride, most conversations I have had with Yankees have been non-verbal, with me ending up on my ass. After one such incident, I had picked myself up, dusted myself off, only to be accosted at a later date by another non-verbal communication that arrived at the clubhouse in a paper bag sent by Billy Martin filled with two dead mackerels, which, in fact, spoke volumes. Billy had provided a note in the fragrant brown bag that read, "Put this in your purse, you California faggot!" I thought to myself, "Hey Billy, weren't you born in California, and raised by your grandparents in California because your parents wanted nothing to do with you?"

You certainly can't talk geography with a Yankee fan either. The famous *New Yorker* magazine had a cover that showed Manhattan, the Hudson River, New Jersey, and then China. In other words to the egocentric mind of a New Yorker there is not much outside of Manhattan. Funny thing, Yankee Stadium is east of Manhattan in the Bronx, and in this book you will find the English translation of the Dutch word for Bronx.

Don't tell a Yankee fan to "get lost," as he probably already is. The difference in language is apparent also when you talk about the ball field. For instance, the Red Sox play in what John Updike referred to as a "lyric little bandbox." The Yankees play in a stadium. Christians go to the lions in a stadium. Actually, the lions play in Detroit, but that's another book!

The authors, throughout this book, see very little similarity between Red Sox fans and Yankee fans, but I see both types of fans that want their hometown to win. The Yankee fan wants their team to win at any cost, the see the end as always justifying the means. I think the rest of the fans of baseball, including Red Sox fans, see it as in the eyes of author sportswriter Grantland Rice, who said, "Be not concerned with winning or losing, but how you play the game!" I say remember, all fans have 98.4 percent in common with chimps. Have a nice talk!

Bill Lee
Craftsbury, Vermont

ACKNOWLEDGMENTS

Thank you to all those baseball fans who shared their thoughts and opinions whether they ended up in the final version or not. Specifically, in no particular order:

Bill Lee, Jimmy Dunn, Jim McCue, Sue B. Doo, Julie Wiskirchen, Steve "Tweed Coat" Hanna, Jacques Altounian, Patrick Freeman, Gary Bradley, Steve Lee, Dave Wolthoff, Rocky LaPorte, Dobie Maxwell, "Yukon" Pete Deisroth, Stratton Mountain School, Kerry Connelly, Julie Honadel, Jennifer Ann, Wayne Previdi, Mark Wolkon, Courtney at Metis Communications, Jonathan Sroka, Jon Fox/Comedy Underground Seattle for always coming through, and the people of LRN for their support and friendship.

A very special thanks to Gillian Mackenzie for her creative input; Paul D'Angelo for his hours of labor; Phil and Murph who influenced (read: provoked) us to write the book; Andy's uncles Eddie, Hy, and Al, cousin Jonathan, and grandfather for introducing him to and cultivating his interest in baseball; Mother Wasif for being an optimistic beacon; Rick's sister Kellie for not calling until the game is over; and to all our friends and family who have tolerated our mood-swings and fleeting social calendar during our months of hibernation to finish this book.

Finally, thanks to Jim Riordan and Heather Buchman and all of Seven Locks Press for their expert guidance in bringing this project to the page.

INTRODUCTION

First off, thank you for your purchase of *How to Talk to a Yankee Fan*. As you've opened the book, we can only assume you're a true baseball fan, (read: Yankee-hater) or a Yankee fan being held at gunpoint and forced to read the pages within, possibly by a Red Sox, Angels, or Mets fan. Either way, we can promise that you will be a better person once you've perused this prose, if only because it'll keep you away from porn sites for a brief spell. Also because you are about to take a giant step forward toward détente and understanding of that classic brute, the Yankee fan (*Biggus Mouthicus*).

Within the covers of this book, the authors will attempt to walk you through the troublesome dealings with said fans. Unless you've been living in a Tora Bora cave for the last century and didn't already know, they're some of the most arrogant, obnoxious, and misanthropic philistines this side of Stalingrad. (*The Yankee fans, not the authors.*)

So, what can you expect to learn from this book? After years of suffering the quintessential Yankee fan, it's finally taken the concerted effort from the newly-formed *How to Talk to a Yankee Fan Institute (or HTTTYF)*, in Cooperstown, New York, to gather the facts and produce for you the most comprehensive instructional manual out there today for communicating with them. By breaking down speech patterns, thought processes, and rhetoric, conversations with Yankee fans will become, at the very least, tolerable. Backed by stats, stories, perceptions, and actual dialogue, everything about a Yankee fan will be stripped down to the bone so you'll always be able to think one step ahead of those pinstriped pinheads.

How often have you been forced to listen to a Yankee fan's insufferable rantings, unintelligent comments, and incessant blathering, leaving you to shake your head in disgust and utter, "typical Yankee fan"? Are you sick and tired of being beaten over the head with their hypocrisy and rhetorical war cry, "Come back and talk to us when you have twenty-six championships"? And how many of these exchanges have ended with you either blue in the face or black in the eye? If your answer is, "Too damn many!" then you've pulled up to the right book.

Believe it or not, we're not doing this to incite more hatred. On the contrary, we feel by opening your eyes to all the mistruths and false beliefs Yankee fans possess, we'll be able to meet them on the field of discourse and sportsmanship instead of angst and rancor. Can't we all just get along? (Okay, we were drinking a *lot* when we wrote this. But really, it could happen. Seriously . . . Hello . . . anyone . . . is this thing on???)

We're just trying to teach the flocks of Yankee-haters how to endure their presence without starting World War III. For every piece of jumbled logic they give you, we'll provide you with ammunition to retaliate. "If you can't beat 'em on the field, beat 'em in the bar," we always say. Or, as the brilliant philosopher Aristotle once proclaimed, "It is with a clove of vinegar that even the most ardent Yankee fan must eat his mouth." (We've got to check the validity of that quote.)

We also have an objective to reach you Yankee fans too. By reading this tome (upon some cursory research, we were pleasantly surprised to learn that some of you *can* read), you are opening yourselves up to change, to self-improvement, and to the reward of a brighter day. Imagine going to the ballpark without being consumed by hatred of your fellow sport fans, of your fellow Americans; (O

Beautiful) For when we walk alone, we are lonely, (*for spacious skies*) but walk with brothers arm in arm (*for amber waves of grain*) and the glory of the Lord above (*for purple mountain majesties*) does shine on us. And so (*above the fruited plain*) we shall congregate not as regional fans, but as Americans! (*America, America*) Americans who share the same passion for the national game, the history, the emotion, the splendor (*God shed his grace on thee*). Not from a perch above the other, but at the same level, arm in arm, cheering for a spirited contest, (*And crown thy good*) not caring who will win or lose (*for brotherhood*) for we are all brothers cut from the same cloth (*from sea*)— a cloth that is red, white, and blue (*to shining*) and reads "Play ball!" (*sea!*)

[Insert huge applause]

Brings a tear to your eye, doesn't it? Now, with that out of the way, it is our pleasure to present you with your guide to non-violent communication with your rival Yankee fans. (However, should you decide to shun our advice and take a Louisville Slugger to them instead, we absolve ourselves of any and all responsibility.)

CHAPTER ONE—
INSIDE THE BRONX ZOO

Since you're still reading this book, it can be assumed that you've had to endure numerous encounters with Yankee fans. It is a necessary evil baseball fans must tolerate on a regular basis. They're everywhere. They walk amongst us. They're our cousins, our co-workers, our friends, our friend's girlfriends, our next-door neighbors, and, of course, Billy Crystal. And as with any good neighbor (*and Billy Crystal*), you want to greet them with a warm smile and a hot bundt cake as your dog leaves a steamy lawn-biscuit on their front porch.

As Michael Corleone conveyed to Frankie Five-Angels in *The Godfather II*, "My father taught me many things here . . . He taught me 'Keep your friends close but your enemies closer.'" And by this very reasoning, we deem it necessary to dissect and analyze this classic brute from the perspective of other fans, Yankee-haters, and even Yankee fans themselves.

Mind you, there *are* decent, reasonable, and intelligent Yankee fans out there. And perhaps there are also thirsty fish, benevolent Nazis, and men who haven't slept with Paris Hilton . . . yet. At the end of the day, no one really gives a darn about any of 'em. So, we are merely focusing on the archetypal Yankee fan—the type that exemplifies them on the whole.

A QUESTION OF SEMANTICS

Before we proceed, though, we would like to clear one thing up. Like, for instance, we know that one singular Red Sox fan will always be plural. That's just the way it is. If anyone tells you they are a "Red Sock" fan, they aren't. But fans from New York are trickier to label.

Are they Yankee fans OR Yankee̲s fans? We've heard both so we decided to go right to the source. We asked a die-hard his thoughts. Never let it be said we disrespected them by calling them the wrong name.

> I'm a Yankee fan. There is no such thing as a "Yankee̲s fan." The comparison to the name for the assholes who share allegiance to the Sox is not an apples-to-apples comparison because the "x" pluralization of "Sox" makes the singular sound so awkward that it is no longer a viable name. For instance, Michael Kay, the horrific Yankee broadcaster, often uses the term "Red Sock." That alone makes that word unusable. But I reiterate— there is no such thing as Yankee̲s fan. I will not argue about this. And I don't want to hear about "long-suffering Red Sox fans" ever again. When you've had to endure sixteen years (and counting) of John Sterling broadcasting your games, come back and talk to me. It took him all of one batter to lose me for the season. That guy is lame!
>
> — *Phil, Yankee fan, Southeastern CT*

So there you have it, they are *"Yankee* fans." And what a Yankee fan he is; our first harmless question to him and he somehow manages to compare losing eighty-six years in a row to listening to an inept announcer muff a call. That seems uh . . . fair? A more succinct response like the following would've done just fine:

> I'm a Yank̲e̲e̲ fan. The one I like is Bernie Williams.
>
> — *Mike M, Concord, NH*

Though it "cannot be argued," according to Phil, it is highly disputed. Even Yankee fans can't agree amongst themselves.

I always say Yankees fan. That is what seems to make the most sense. If you cheer for the *team*, then it is Yankees. If you cheered for only one player, then it would be a Yankee player. Even then, I still use Yankees.

— *Brad Turnow, owner/president of The Sports Palace, Inc., specializing in New York Yankees memorabilia*

Now, who are we supposed to believe? The owner of a sports memorabilia operation or a fan with an obvious distaste for polite disagreement and the Boston Red Sox? Well, in the interest of writing less and saving trees, we'll go with "Yank*ee*" fan throughout the book.

EVOLUTION OF THE YANKEE FAN

Over the past several years, the debate rages on over whether Yankee fans evolved or were created by some deity—call it "unintelligent design"—as a kind of practical joke to all HIS other creations.

The revelations behind the evolution of Yankee fans are still an inexact science. Geneticists, biochemists, and design theorists all have spent countless days and nights working toward the answer of how a Yankee fan came to be.

Several clues had been revealed and mislabeled. It has always been assumed that Yankee fans evolved directly from Ramapithecus, a species that for many years was widely recognized as a direct ancestor of humans. Through that misinterpretation, many experts hunted for what was called the "missing link" to try to connect the creature with what we are familiar with in this day and age.

Ramapithecus was then established to be an extinct type of orangutan. That finding, coupled with the first ability to do DNA testing in 1953, allowed the so-called Bottleheimer Theory to develop, postulating that Ramapithecus did not, in fact, become extinct, but evolved into a special breed, unique in its characteristics to all other organisms—the Yankee fan.

For nearly five decades, top geneticists have floated the Dingleberger Theory at conventions worldwide. But that all changed when Dr. Franz Hoffenhoffen attended a game at Yankee Stadium during the World Genomics Forum in New York City during the summer of 2001. He observed that Yankee fans spend a great deal of time hunched over scratching their armpits, crotches, and hindquarters followed by a furtive sniff of their fingers (an action that caused one fan to fall off his seat).

He further noted these fans were prone to throwing various objects such as pretzels, beer, popcorn, metal projectiles, and the like, much the same way that orangutans throw their own feces. (Though rare, something Yankee fans have done as well.)

Dr. Hoffenhoffen informed his fellow scientists of his breakthrough later that night. Though they didn't *immediately* take him seriously (he was still covered in mustard and beer from the game), one thesis paper later proved all the evidence that was needed.

Because of this evolutionary glitch, the Yankee fan remains far behind other species on the evolutionary scale. And since we interact with them so often, we've had to become skilled in learning how to cope with them. We'll begin with a detailed illustration of a

FUN FACT:

The average human is made up of 90 percent water; the average Yankee Fan is made up of 84 percent Miller Genuine Draft.

Yankee fan's brain because, as in *Planet of the Apes*, in order to be able to communicate with them, we must first try to understand them.

DIAGRAM OF A TYPICAL YANKEE FAN'S BRAIN

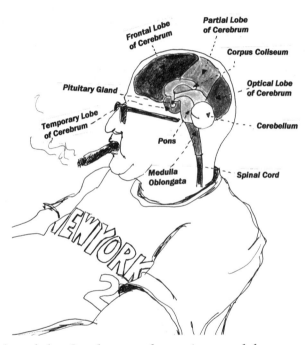

Frontal Lobe of the Cerebrum - the region used for reasoning and judgment. Typically one-third the size of the average human being.

Pituitary Gland - a gland attached to base of brain that secretes greasy testosterone through their pores.

Temporal Lobe of the Cerebrum - region containing centers of hearing and recall (overloaded with numbers "1918," "26," and "61*").

Pons - the part of brain that realizes the true self. It is buried deep within the Cerebrum and is rarely accessible during a conscious state.

Medulla Oblongata - controls automatic functions including irregular heartbeats. Keeps blood pumping at a steady 10°F.

Parietal Lobe of the Cerebrum - vital sensory centers that automatically force them to complain whenever team loses two games in a row.

Corpus Callosum - a grossly oversized collection of nerve strands that manages self-image.

Occipital Lobe of the Cerebrum - houses the centers of vision and speech. Less developed than most mammals. Capable of storing few words, mainly "$#^@*!"

Cerebellum - the part of the brain that regulates balance, posture, movement, and all motor skills, (i.e., giving the finger).

Spinal Cord - a very thin bundle of nerve fibers that run through the spine to connect the base of the brain directly to the wallet.

> To your average Yankee-hater, to don that lackluster white-on-black Yankee cap is to announce to the world that not only are you most likely a self-indulgent and obnoxious Neanderthal, but you are apparently rather comfortable with the title.
>
> I picture the stereotypical New Yorker with an Italian accent and greasy, black hair under their Yankee cap. And being very drunk.
>
> — *Mike Felton, Chicago, IL*

> Whenever I see someone sporting a Yankee hat, I immediately think, "There goes a guy who purposely drives slow in the fast lane in heavy traffic, stops at green lights, pushes his way onto the elevator before letting anyone else off, farts, blames it on the guy in the wheelchair, gets off on the next floor, bumps into the delivery guy knocking everything out of his hands, turns to him and says, 'What're *you* lookin' at, dickweed?!'"
>
> — *Larry Repucci, Radio DJ*

Dealing with Yankee fans is often like dealing with non-English speaking people. They speak a different language. In fact, much like the binary system of mathematics, Yankee fans have their own way

> ## FUN FACT:
> *In the late '60s/early '70s, Yankee fans wore different colors when attending games. Their hats were a lighter shade of blue with a narrower "N" and "Y" set on the hat in orange. They revisited this merchandise in 1986 before settling for the retro monochromatic dark blue and white that you see them wearing today.*

of tabulating. At first glance, they might seem random, but upon closer inspection, you'll notice a pattern in the discrepancies.

Why are Yankee fans like this? Well-noted psychologist Johnson McQuardle has been studying their brain for almost a decade and has found them to have unquestionable traits particular only to them and missing from the brain of a regular baseball fan. These traits include:

1) Yankee math reasoning

McQuardle detected an almost dyslexic understanding of basic math and science stemming from their overaggressive temporal lobe as it overrides left brain logic reasoning.

Sample responses by Yankee Fans to McQurdle math survey:

$5 + 9 = 26$

$163 = 1918$

400 divided by $400 = 61*$

9 million—$34{,}000 = 7$

$10 \times 10 = 26$

$710 + 2 = 714$

$710 + 4 = 56$

$x + y = F*** you!$

n^2 = the square root of your mother

Cosine 180 = I got your cosine right here

2) Lacking the part of the brain that controls primitive needs (the id)

Yankee fans have an almost uncanny knack to contort facts to suit their needs. Their statements often contain certain basic truths, but something isn't kosher about how these truths are combined.

Case study:

> In 2001, the Red Sox and Dodgers had a higher payroll than the Yankees.
>
> — *B. Rosenberg, New Hampton, NY*

As you'll see in Chapter Eleven, that statement is false. But Yankee fan B. Rosenberg has the basic elements correct—"the Red Sox," "the Dodgers," and "the Yankees." All are teams. All had a payroll. And our records indicate that 2001 was, in fact, a year. So where did the statement veer from accuracy? Is it possible that the Yankee fan *wanted* to believe that his team had not outspent all other teams as it does, year after year, and in effect, *accidentally* inverted the truth?

It's possible that he used a source that had the specifics wrong. In this day and age of information overload, there is a great likelihood that some "professional" bloggers and/or journalists misspoke. B. Rosenberg's only fault here is in neglecting to check his fact before stating it. It's similar to "cherry picking" information, a tactic popular with "certain administrations" in high public office. Or the more cynical view: the Yankee fan may have purposefully misrepresented the facts, otherwise known as lying, in the hope that you wouldn't research its validity. McQuardle attributes this behavior to an extremely underdeveloped temporal lobe of the cerebrum, leaving it without a moral compass or *id*, as Freud would say.

3) Ignorance

As you can see from the diagram on page five, the occipital lobe, the lobe that controls speech, is spaced further apart from the frontal lobe, the reasoning center, than normal humans; thus preventing logic from reaching the vocal center before something is said. McQuardle reasoned that this was how the Yankee fan can say anything with no basis or understanding of it. Take for example when a Yankee fan chided Laurie Russo in June of 1996 about her beloved Mets' misfortune:

Yankee Fan: "Ha, ha, ha . . . the Mets haven't won in what, like, ten years!"

Laurie: "Uh, the Yankees haven't won it in EIGHTEEN!"

[*blank stare from obviously uninformed bandwagon-jumper*]

At that point, Dr. Evil entered and said, "You just don't get it, do you, Scott?"

4) Socially obnoxious behavior

An EKG of a Yankee fan's brain revealed an interesting phenomenon to McQuardle—the cerebellum pinches a drooping corpus callosum, causing movement and actions to occur with no level of decorum.

Shortly after Grady Little had been banished from Boston in November 2003, Sox superfan, Kate DiStefano, was finally getting married following a long engagement. After the ceremony, as they were getting into the limo, her best friend's husband (a Yankee lover) couldn't miss the opportunity to take a shot at the bride. He turned to her and said, "Well, at least one of the things we thought would never happen just did. Too bad for the Red Sox though."

That was cold. Cameras were on them and everything. Yet she bit her tongue as she wished he would contract scabies on his "wedding tackle."

McQuardle writes in his thesis, "Without the ability for their brain synapses to fire properly having been damaged from years of hearing

'Theeeeeeeeeeeeeee YANKEES win!!! Theeeeeeeeeeeeeee YANKEES win!!!' a resulting void is created in the part of the brain that handles interpersonal relations. Therefore, the inherent, physiological defects in Yankee fans' brains make it difficult, often times impossible, for the average, non-Yankee fan to engage them in meaningful, logical, and pleasant conversation, often leaving said fan with much mental anguish."

The following are selected excerpts that the *How to Talk to a Yankee Fan Institute* collected from hundreds of Yankee-haters through a series of interviews. We all know that a writer's natural proclivity is to embellish stories to enhance the comedic and/or dramatic effect, but please be aware that we here the Institute are reporting the truth, the whole truth, and nothing but the truth, so help us Teddy Ballgame. All we did was supply the questions. The responses of the non-Yankee fans speak volumes.

WHAT IS THE GENERAL FEELING YOU GET WHEN TALKING TO A YANKEE FAN?

Car-sickness.

— *Brian Wurschum, New York, NY*

Pure hatred. I've actually caught myself daydreaming about the mathematical probability of a mid-air collision between the Yankees and Lakers team airplanes.

— *Bill Burr, comedian/actor*

Talking to a Yankee fan is like talking to a mix of a block of wood, a communist loyalist, and the enforcer for a street gang. Like a block of wood, they can't comprehend simple logic and will cast aside any basic argument that you make simply because they don't understand. Like a communist loyalist, they are completely blinded to the truth and won't even entertain the notion that the Yankees might not be perfect in every way. And like the enforcer of a local street gang, they will physically attack you if you look at them the wrong way.

— *AV, Mets fan*

I hate them with such a deep passion. If it's the Yanks versus the S.S., I'm screaming, "Himmler, take third!!!"

— *Matthew Kupferberg, dreamer*

I just don't understand them. They are not rational, nice people. They have mental disorders that prevent them from realizing how annoying they are.

— *A.J. Poulin, Los Angeles*

Just pity. Pure, plain pity. They're so used to winners being bought for them that they forget that real fans have to suffer through those "rebuilding," years when the roster reads more like a comedy lineup than a baseball lineup.

— *Adam Sivits, Brooklyn, NY*

I generally feel like I'm talking to someone who is close-minded, naïve, delusional, arrogant, and hides behind chest-thumping machismo to conceal a disturbing lack of intelligence and morals.

— *Ben Hill, NYC*

A mix of pity and disgust. I think individually they're an insecure lot. They feel very small as people, so they cling to their monuments and their "rings" as proof that they are somebody. I've never heard so many people take so much credit for so little that's happened on their watch. Mostly, they're sad people trying to pump themselves up.

— *Greg Prince, Mets fan*

They are bandwagon-jumping front-runners with $16.95 in their pocket to buy a hat. The true-blue, knowledge-able Yankee fans I view with a small amount of respect and a great deal of disdain.

— *Andrew Polmer*

Yankee fans are nothing more than droids playing "Follow the Leader." Root for the behemoth and buy into all the best marketing that money can buy. Generally, I find them uninformed regarding any team, any player, or anything outside of the Bronx. They believe twenty-six World Series titles justifies their allegiance to the team regardless of whatever they do.

— *Matt Kennedy Wood-Ridge, NJ*

I mostly get nauseated when talking to Yankee fans. They just don't seem to get it. How many movies have they made of rich kids versus kids from the "other side of the tracks?" And how many times do you root for the rich kids? Never! So why root for the Yankees?

— *BJ Cook, Chateaugay, NY*

I wouldn't root for them if they were playing a bunch of convicts who mugged my mother at gunpoint. And to be quite honest with you, neither would she.

— *Anon*

It's hard to blame the last respondent for wanting his or her identity protected . . . at least until the trial is over.

HOW MUCH DO YANKEE FANS RUB IT IN WHEN YOUR TEAM LOSES?

Not so much a rub as it is a stomp, or a deep-tissue-ing.

— *Adam Sivits*

Their stock move is to roll their eyes and say things like, "When will you learn; you will never beat us." That over the top, highbrow attitude is exactly why I hate their fans as much as I hate the team itself.

— *Matt Kennedy, Wood-Ridge, NJ*

Enough to make me want to beat them with their own arm.

— *Luis Blanco*

It's more about our troubles instead of their success, which makes it more annoying. They get more joy seeing another fan unhappy than them actually being happy about their team.

— *Dustin Millman, YES Network*

Walking through the streets and subways of New York after the first three Sox losses in the '04 ALCS, I received lots of cocky jeers, like "Ha! Better luck next time, guys!"

Even a homeless man yelled, "Red Sox SUCK!" when he saw my hat. I gave him a penny.

— *Ryan Walker, Ocean Grove, NJ*

I have a friend who is a big Yankee fan. Every October during the World Series, he would send me an envelope in the mail. I'd open it up and the only thing inside would be three baseball cards: Bob Stanley, Mookie Wilson, and Bill Buckner. I never understood why he would be compelled to do this.

— *Angelica Fisichella*

We would, Angela. It's simple: Yankee fans are, as Mark Ratner said to Mike Demone in *Fast Times at Ridgemont High*, "Rude, crude, and socially unacceptable!" Let us remind you readers that there are exceptions to the rule. We're dealing in generalities here, albeit generalities representing the majority.

Now what kind of authors would we be if we didn't give a Yankee fan the floor? Ladies and gentlemen, all the way from the Bronx, wearing the pinstriped pajamas, we give you . . .

Aw, c'mon! I'm a Yankee fan, and we're not that bad. In my experience, it's more dangerous for a Yankee fan to go to Fenway (where I've seen fights break out) than to be a Sox fan at "the Stadium." I've actually had pleasant trips to the Bronx sitting next to Sox fans. Maybe things will calm down now that Red Sox Nation has a ring again. Anyway, Yankee fans are good fans. But good luck with your book though.

— *Josh Catone*

Thank you, Mr. Catone. I'm sure other fans feel as though it's Christmas and their birthday all in one each time they visit "the

Stadium." Perhaps you might take a gander at Chapter Five: The Bad, the Worse, and the Ugly. And isn't it rather presumptuous of Yankee fans to always refer to Yankee Stadium simply as, "*the* Stadium"—as if it was the *only* stadium in the sporting world? These are the same people who refer to New York City merely as "*the* City." By using that Yankee logic, the authors would now just refer to *How to Talk to a Yankee Fan* simply as, "*the* Book!"

LIST THE FIRST THREE ADJECTIVES THAT COME TO MIND TO DESCRIBE A YANKEE FAN:

If you talk to enough people, as we have, you'll begin to see redundancies. Yankee fans are of a certain ilk. They can be described creatively or in a more erudite fashion, but it all comes down to the fact that they are—well, feel free to use any or all of the adjectives below when describing them . . .

Abhorrent, Appalling, Annoying, *Arrogant*, Belligerent, Brainwashed, Brash, Cantankerous, Cocky, Condescending, Contemptible, Corrupt, Cruel, Culpable, Deceitful, Depraved, Despicable, Devious, Dirty, Disgraceful, Disgusting, Drunk, Egotistical, Evil, Excruciating, Fair-weather, Fetid, Foolish, Fraudulent, Front-running, Gangrenous, Gluttonous, Godforsaken, Greasy, Haughty, Hideous, Ignorant, Immoral, Insipid, Insufferable, Intolerable, Jerky, Loathsome, Loud, Moronic, Nasty, Nauseating, Nefarious, Obnoxious, Oblivious, Pathetic, Quarrelsome, Rank, Rapacious, Repellent, Reprehensible, Repugnant, Rude, Sadistic, Self-righteous, Shameless, Smelly, Smug, Spoiled, Squalid, Swarthy, Trite, Unbearable, Uncultured, Uninformed, Vile, Voracious, Weasely, Xenophobic, Yapping, YIDDISH, Zootrophic—(*Look it up, ya mulyaks!*)

Why did we highlight "arrogant"? Ask Jon Neuhaus why he started rooting for the Yankees and he'll tell ya, "Because I am a red-blooded, God-fearing, patriotic American. The Yankees are America."

Still wondering about that little "arrogant" characterization?

After all of this abuse, we thought it benevolent to end the chapter with a story that comes directly off the #4 train, from the poison pen of a Yankee fan. This yarn was included because we felt it was the perfect example to depict what a true blue Yankee fan is really like and just how difficult it has been for the *How to Talk to a Yankee Fan Institute* to develop strategies to communicate with them! Regarding their archrival Boston Red Sox, this piece was written shortly after the 2004 ALCS.

THE TURTLE—BY MARK W., YANKEE FAN

We Yankee fans that have managed to acquire Red Sox fan friends walk a slippery slope. We suffer. Sox fans suffer, therefore, so must we. Year upon year we've had to provide a sympathetic shoulder and patient ear to the broken recording of inferiority and heartbreak. Sox fans proclaim a resignation to their lowly state, insist that they are comfortably numb, and then whine incessantly like little bitches. "See, you Yankee fans have no idea what it's like. You can't imagine what we go through every year." And you know what? They're right, we can't.

But as Yankee fan friends of Red Sox fans, at least we try to understand. We try to imagine what it would be like to have to root for a team that sucked that bad, a team so hideously cursed. We ponder the horror of having our hopes and dreams tethered to a band of hopeless losers. It's inconceivable to us; fans whose pedigree of losing dates back almost as far as our pedigree of championships. Still, we take the time. We struggle to break through.

Our Sox fan friends, on the other hand, make no attempt at understanding the pain of the Yankee fan. When we blow a series, they dismiss it with a cavalier, "You'll win it next year," or the old stand-by, "Come on, man . . . twenty-six championships." They cannot imagine our pain, as they feel theirs is obviously so much nobler, being steeped in tradition such as it is.

I put to them this: that not only is our pain valid, it is far greater and nobler than theirs. To be as high and mighty as we Yankee fans are, imagine the plunge we must take when the team lets us down. Of course the Red Sox or Cubs or White Sox or Giants, etc. are gonna let you down. Where's the real anguish in that?

When Rivera hiccupped and we went on to lose the 2001 World Series to Arizona, after every last Yankee fan had put that one in the bag; that was *anguish*. That was "dead grandma" anguish. And when we blew the 3–0 lead in this last series, when we blew the historical lock that was "dead mom" anguish. When the Sox lose, what is that? That's "dead turtle" anguish. You just get another turtle and it's gonna die next year. You know it, and your folks know it. How hard is that pain?

It's five months later, and I still haven't recovered from Game Seven. I lost a little piece of myself that day, and I believe so did the universe. But I give you Red Sox fans fair warning—after eighty-some years of dead turtles, you now have an iguana. And when that thing dies, you're going to get your first real taste of Yankee pain.

Evidently, the "universe" is a Yankee fan, according to Mr. W. We wonder what anguish Cub fans or Brewers fans are subjected to—dead skin cell anguish?

And so there lays the great disconnect between Yankee fans and all other fans. We've never lost our grandmother and for that, we're grateful. Hey, since she's still around, let's ask *her* for a pearl of wisdom regarding what she thinks of Yankee fans.

> They're arrogant bastards.
>
> — *Grandma Davidson*

Your Honor, on behalf of all baseball fans, in the matter of *The American People vs. New York*, the prosecution happily and respectfully, rests its case.

CHAPTER TWO—
BREEDS OF YANKEE FANS

Lest we be accused of stereotyping all Yankee fans into one pod of offensiveness, there are, in fact, many different types of the species, though the majority of them share in common the attributes previously mentioned. To the outsider, those adorned in Yankee paraphernalia are all similar; it is only the astute observer that can recognize the subclasses in the family of Yankee fans. Some saw DiMaggio play live and some make Raider fans look "comfortably well-adjusted."

By spending days upon days at "the Stadium," gathering anecdotes from other fans, and poring through hours of security videotape and police records, our institute has established descriptive characterizations of each specific type of Yankee fan and has recorded sightings of these various breeds across the globe. See if you can identify anyone from that last game you attended.

(For your assistance, we've graded them on the "Louisville Slugger Scale" which represents the number of times you'd want to crown each type with said bat. Each number is only a suggestion. Feel free to adjust according to your own taste.)

JERSEY MALL RATS
Overview

Straight out of Asbury Park, these permanently-trapped-in-the-'80s, mullet-haired, gum-snappin', bench- pressin', gold chain-wearin' mall rats punch out from their assistant manager post at the Chess King, tighten the drawstring on their painter's pants, hop in their IROC Z-28, crank up Bon Jovi's *Slippery When Wet* on the cassette player and head over to "*the* Stadium."

Pre-game Rituals

Once in their car, they jump on the Garden State Parkway, beeline it over the George Washington, and finally skid into an overpriced Yankee Stadium parking garage. It is here where they'll meet up with fellow cretins Joey, Robbie, and Nicky. (Nicky always gets great scalped seats from his cousin, "Bronx Tony"). Each armed with a well-concealed bottle of Schnapps, they quickly "burn a J" and make their way into the stadium just in time for the first pitch.

How to Spot Them

You're actually more likely to smell them before you even see 'em coming, for they are perpetually surrounded by a thin cloud of Polo cologne; quite possibly the only fragrance of its ilk strong enough to

> **FUN FACT:**
> *Statistics show that four out of every ten of the subspecies Jersey Mallrat get nailed for OUI on the way back to Jersey. (Remember to watch for the PD on the Major Deegan Expressway.)*

cut through the regular stadium stench of stale beer and ass. But, not necessarily more welcome.

How to Talk to Them

Jersey Mallrats are among the most obnoxious Yankee fans—which, in itself, speaks volumes. Should you be so unfortunate to have to sit near these buffoons, you're in for a *loooong* night. Their typical game "to do list" reads as follows:

1. Stand up for the whole game giving everyone behind them an "obstructed view" seat.
2. Sit down only between innings to furtively sneak sips of Schnapps.
3. Scream obscenities.
4. Try to get crowd to partake in idiotic chants like, "Douchebag! Douchebag! Douchebag!" and "Fuck the ump! Fuck the ump! . . . "

When they confront you with their standby, "What are you lookin' at, dickweed?!" as they inevitably will, pretend you only speak French. They'll bombard you with xenophobic slurs but you won't have to respond to them because, after all, you can't understand them. You're French, remember?

Slugger Rating 🏏🏏🏏🏏🏏 as a warm-up.

GECKOS

Overview

No, a Gecko is not an iguana who sells car insurance. Geckos are named after Michael Douglas' character in *Wall Street*. They are the soul-less, white-collar professionals such as investment bankers, lawyers, stockbrokers, and "business consultants" who revel in impenitent materialism having come to NY to fulfill their favorite pastime— greed. You'll see them at every game (though usually not before the third inning and, if the Yanks are losing, not long after the sixth).

Weeknight Game Attire

Basically the same after-work casual street clothes they wear on weekends; their requisite Yankee hat with Yankee watch to compliment their Dockers khaki's and collared shirt with the top two buttons undone. Real hellcats.

Psychology

Geckos take great pride in being a Yankee fan ever since it first occurred to them. (Typically the day they got hired at their investment bank.) They seek out anything that grants them "in crowd" status among friends, co-workers and, most importantly, the boss.

Their company has season tickets to Yankee Stadium so this breed merely uses their "allegiance" to the team for career advancement. And in order to impress potential clients and business partners, they become a "walking wikipedia" of Yankee knowledge, often cramming for Yankee stats harder than they did for the LSAT's.

How to Talk to Them

It's nearly impossible for them to begin a conversation about baseball with an original thought in their head as their feeble knowledge of Yankee history plagues them. It's much easier for them to repeat something they've overheard at the water cooler like: "I can't believe Williams is batting second today." Or "I wish Mattingly were still on the team."

To interact, just remember to give them a K.I.S.S. (Keep It Simple, Stupid!) Tell them things you're sure they'd understand, like:

- "The Yankees have a long history of playing baseball."
- "Pinstripes are very slimming on the players."
- "George Steinbrenner made a lot of money last year."

Anyway, they're less concerned with you than they are with the Asian businessmen they're schmoozing. They'll spend much of the game as a color commentator while trying to slip in hints about the pending deal.

"Look at that, Mr. Fung-Mao-san; bases loaded with one out and the winning run is coming to the plate. And the ability to deal with a lot on one's *plate* is what we strive for at Grift, Weinberg, and Cheney. Whom better than one of your own, the most honorable Hideki Matsui-san, to win the game for the Yankee-sans? He is worth every yen that George Steinbrenner-san spends on him! We say '*Domo arigato*' to you for sending him to us! Come on Godzilla!"

Repercussions

It doesn't really matter that Mr. Fung-Mao is Chinese because his client is mesmerized by the drunk girl in the luxury box who's flashing the crowd. The business deal goes through. The Gecko gets his huge bonus and continues to have life open every door for him. Rest assured though, he *will* wind up in hell.

Shmooze Geckos

This is a subset of the typical investment banker Gecko species. They're in sales. Be wary of them. They will try to relate to everyone and everything. They're Yankee fans, but they're also a fan of every other team out there. Go to buy a used car wearing an Expos jersey and they have a favorite aunt who summered in Montreal once so he loves the Expos. Drink a cup of Starbucks coffee and they become big Seattle Mariners fans. Usually, they'll get a vital piece of baseball information wrong. It's not even worth correcting them when they say they love everything about Philadelphia, especially Wrigley Field. Just walk away.

Slugger rating   ⚾ ⚾ ⚾   (Add three more if they have Michael Douglas' entire acting resume committed to memory.)

JECKYLS

Overview

Underneath those reasonable exteriors are the illogical fans that you suspected they might be, but you only see it if there's a game on. They're generally good fans who know the players and appreciate the sport . . . until the first pitch is thrown. Every conversation you have with these subliminal demons appears rational and intriguing on the surface. Pre-game, they'll make great sense on some of the deeper issues you breached regarding the state of the game as a whole and even concede a few of your points. But during the game, beware: they will sucker-punch you with their rhetoric.

Game Habits

They begin yelling at the screen and at anyone who dares to question them. They see strikes when the whole world sees balls. They cannot be made happy without full and utter annihilation of the opponent; something where the other team slumps off the field weeping after having soiled themselves collectively. Anything short of that is a catastrophe. They couldn't care less if the Yankees played themselves in a split squad World Series. As long as their team wins, they still brag about the championship count.

Transformation Process

When the lights go up on the Stadium, Jeckyls began to gasp and wheeze, falling to their knees as their body morphs into some horrific creature with fangs and glowing, yellow eyes and hair on their knuckles (though many Yankee fans already have that). That's when the Yankee monster is revealed. They may not even be watching the game, but somehow, they can sense it. Get away from them! Run!

The change is instantaneous. Circa 1998: "I think it would be kinda nice to see the Padres win this year. We've had our time. They deserve it as much as any—[Padres Manager Bruce] BOCHY OPENS HIS F***N' MOUTH ONE MORE TIME AT THE UMP, I HOPE HE GETS HIS F***N' FACE SMASHED IN!!! HEY, BLUE, THAT WAS A GREAT CALL—YOU F***N' ****BAG.

How to Talk to Them
Prepare to combat these customary expressions:

- That's f***n' bull****!
- No f***n' way!
- You're f***n' killin' me!
- I don't f***n' believe it!
- Can you f***n' believe that?
- This is un-f***n'-believable!
- Aw, c'mon!

Slugger Rating /////// It takes a lot to calm them down.

TEARJERKER JERKS
Overview
Yankee fans who *swear* they feel bad for you and your team and really hope you win someday, but are only hiding the fireworks display and tickertape parade going off in their heart for your team's misfortune. They spend so much time concealing their joy for your pain that they typically pull a groin trying not to gloat. They are similar to the Jeckyls, but are sweeter in a fake way.

What to Look For

There's a certain condescending arrogance in their kindness. They've been through this before so they know they can show a little sympathy for you and still end up contented in the end. Whether it's an early season slump or a heated playoff race, they know that their team's mighty payroll will prevail. After all, that's what money does; in addition to buying happiness, it solves problems.

It's tough to see the jerkiness on the outside of a Tearjerker Jerk. They usually hide this trait underneath a façade of humanity. It'll come out in subtle ways like their sorrowfully tilting their head after the Yankees win and saying, "Phew! Looks like we pulled that one out after all. I was worried. Your team put up a good fight though. You should be proud." That compassionate gesture makes it seem like they care about your feelings.

Favorite Hobbies

Convincing you that they're not the "bad Yankee fans" and that they're pulling for your team almost as much as they're pulling for their own.

How to Talk to Them

They can't grasp the concept that other teams can't keep up with the Yankees. They drink "Steinbrenner Stoli" and now see the world through pinstriped glasses. They have been raised all-things Yankee and it would take an enormous undertaking or one major or traumatic event to get them to see the light. At least they're nice people about it, which is what makes talking to them so painful. Pop a couple of Quaaludes and a shot or two of whiskey before dealing with them.

Slugger Rating / / But be compassionate about it.

BANDWAGON BI-YATCHES

Overview

These are, hands-down, among the worst types of Yankee fans: the superficial, ignorant, bandwagon women who claim allegiance to the Yanks simply by wearing a Yankee hat because it showcases their "ultra chic, casual-yet-classy look." They don't really know anything about the Yankees and they don't *really* care about the Yankees. They couldn't name more than three players on any current Yankees roster if their lives depended on it.

"Let's see . . . there's Derek Jeter! Sooo hot! And um . . . A-Rod. That's two! And . . . oh, I miss Andy Pettite, but I know he went to some other stupid team so, I'd say . . . um, you know, that black guy who goes on right after Jeter."

Some were Prom Queen. Some were runners-up in the *Miss Teen USA* pageant. Some were the cheerleaders everyone in high school wanted to nail but never could. These young women were not interested in *high school* boys. Eeew! Instead, they sought the attention of

older men; namely Mr. Ramsey, the substitute English Lit teacher (*who actually did nail them*).

Background

They grew up in the ultra-conservative, wealthy, and white suburbs located far away from Yankee Stadium. For their "sweet sixteen" they received a SAAB Turbo 900. By age twenty-one (or third SAAB, whichever came first) they've built strong résumés with impressive job skills:

27

Woodland Hills Animal Shelter	Volunteer Care Giver	1993—1997
Yearbook Committee	Photo Editor	1996—2000
Prom Committee	Music Coordinator	1999—2000
Food & Beverage Specialist	La Strada Ristorante	June 2000
Actress	Arby's commercial	July 2000

Secret Desires

Eventually, they all flock to Hollywood to become a model/actress/singer/PETA spokesperson. They dedicate their spare time to "curing world hunger, saving the whales, and spreading peace and spiritual harmony throughout the universe." But most wind up at a "Bring Your Own Steroid" party at the Playboy Mansion locked in a three-way with Jose Canseco and two minor leaguers to be named later.

Psychology—Not true fans, they mock the very essence of the game by putting on the Yankee cap. They don't watch games on TV or read the sports pages (or anything else outside of *Vogue*, for that matter). They don't go to games unless it's the post-season or they get invited to a coke party in P. Diddy's luxury box suite or both. They feign loyalty to the Yanks for two reasons: 1) They always win. 2) Jeter's ass! *(not necessarily in that order)*.

How to Talk to Them

While the women at *HTTTYF* feel they don't have to put up with these fans, the *HTTTYF* men realize that they must, unfortunately, put up with them. Why? Because bi-yatches are hot. Wicked hot.

Slugger Rating 🏏 🏏 🏏 🏏 🏏 and, for good measure. 🏏

MAFIOSO MEATBALLS

Overview

Pick any Italian-American stereotype and you'll nail this type of Yankee fan on the head. However, use extreme caution when doing so or you'll likely wind up at the bottom of the Hudson River. These are guys named Pasquale, Giuseppe, Vincenzo, Salvatore, Bruno Fingers, Uncle V, and Bronx Tony (aka "The Ticket Master"). They are mostly from the Bronx and Brooklyn.* Due in part to their proximity, they are among some of the few true-blue, die-hard Yankee fans.

Many who resided in the Flatbush section of Brooklyn circa 1957 still cling to the Dodgers, who fled legendary Ebbets Field for browner pastures in smog-riddled Los Angeles that following season.

Psychology

They have an innate "past is prologue" mindset: Their grandfathers lived through racial persecution when they first stepped off the boat from the Mother Country. Their fathers lived through the Great Depression in the 1930s. They lived through the Drought" from 1978-1996. And through all this hardship, nothing has been more important than "la famiglia," including the Yankees.

Distinguishing Characteristics

We're not sure. We don't dare look in their direction for too long. Eh, we didn't see nuthin'! *Capisce*?!

Baseball Q Rating

High. When brought in for questioning, they often "can't remember" what happened to Dominic "the Weasel" Scarboni last Tuesday night, but can recall every piece of Yankee history including stats, standings, and players past and present. More importantly, they know the game.

Ballpark Behavior

They actually don't attend many games, preferring the comforts of the neighborhood bar to the many discomforts of Yankee Stadium. When they do go to the game, they're surprisingly taciturn. They keep to themselves and rarely revel in victories.

How to Talk to Them

For the most part, they are great baseball fans. They don't continually shove the Yankees past accomplishments down your throat. They don't chant "1918" or wear "Long Live the Curse" T-shirts. They simply love the game. In their world "respect" is everything and, naturally, a two-way street. Sure, if provoked, they can be bold and opinionated, but they have earned that right for the following reasons:

1. They're local boys rooting for the hometown team.
2. You gonna tell 'em otherwise?

Slugger Rating

Um, with all due respect, we'll let this one go. In fact, we'll give *ourselves* just to appease them.

FRIGGIN' UTES

Overview

They're the *youth* at the games cursing up a storm and offending everyone in sight as their proud parents sit by idly, often encouraging and rewarding their behavior. "Look honey, our little boy just dropped his first f-bomb. Good boy, Billy. Here's a crunchy ginger snap for ya."

Age/Sex

They're easy to spot; look for early teens all the way down to toddlers just barely able to form a sentence. The real "potty-mouths" are primarily male. The female of the species mostly just give the finger.

Psychology

Just as pit bulls—generally great dogs that only turn evil if trained as such—so, too, is the Yankee fan. As children, they don't know enough to think for themselves and rely on what they hear around them. The blame lies strictly on the parents' dandruff-covered shoulders. If not kept in check, Utes will blithely continue this behavior right into adulthood. Once an asshole, always an asshole.

Physiology

Look for the glazed-over, Damien from *The Omen* eyes, the slight spittle coming out of their mouths, and the sloppy attire. An early-onset unibrow is not uncommon.

Hobbies

Outside of "the Stadium" these kids engage in a number of after-school activities such as: model airplane stomping, scaring pigeons, frying ants with a magnifying glass, and pulling legs off daddy long legs, mosquitoes, and the neighbor's cat. Their favorite game is "hide and pray we don't find you or else you're in for a serious beat-down."

How to Talk to Them

Utes have a limited vocabulary. Their first word is generally preceded by an expletive as in, "[bleepin'] mama." They're not overly big, though their jaws can actually unhinge and expand like an African boa constrictor for the evolutionary purpose of yelling louder than their small stature should allow. This is largely due to the fact that as children, instead of a pacifier, they teethed on a block of wood.

The rhetoric they routinely spew is duplicitous. These kids will mock the Angels for never winning (though they've won more recently than the Yankees). They make fun of the Mets for "buying all their players" and they still consider the Diamondbacks an expansion franchise though the team is older than they themselves are. What they need is a good deprogrammer. *See Chapter Fourteen— Deyankifying the Masses*

Slugger Rating (for them) (for their parents).

OUT-OF-TOWNIES
Overview

They've been Yankee fans for years, but they've left NY. So there's no one place where you'll find them. It could be in a line at the post office in Elko, Nevada, in the dentist's chair in Aberdeen, South Dakota, or delivering your new couch in Couchdeliveryville, Maryland.

The worst of these types are the ones who never lived in NY in the first place. Oh, but they have an aunt who once dated a guy whose cousin knows this kid who saw Ferris pass out at *31* Flavors and is also a Yankee fan; so they're *deeply* connected to the team.

How to Spot Them

You won't find out they're a Yankee fan unless both (a) there's something to alert them to your baseball allegiance and (b) the Yankees are currently ranked higher than your team in the standings, have beaten them recently, or have a better history than them (which narrows it down to include uh, EVERY other team).

They are prone to traveling alone, but won't hesitate to rub in any failure of your team or spew hypocritical rhetoric. They eschew public decorum at the game and will yell things like, "Throw it at his head!" to quell homesickness, then dismiss any offended spectators around them with a pointed, "Mind your damn business or I'll crack you right in the pie-hole!"

Psychology

If the Yankees are doing well, then everyone has to know that they're Yankee fans. Should the Yankees falter, they don't think much about the team. Their excuse is that the local newspaper doesn't cover New York sports so why should they care? There's a thought-process that goes on in these fans' heads: in order to decide to go to a game simply to root *against* both teams, all their other options for the day must be exhausted. So they go down a checklist:

"What should I do today? I could kick homeless people. Nah, did that last weekend. How about just shouting insults at people on the beach? I'd have to bring sun block and I am not in the mood. I know, I'll go make fun of those *losers* at the Dodgers-Diamondbacks game!"

Baseball Q Rating

Their baseball IQ is lower than most of the other Yankee fans which means it's pretty darn low. They can pick out which team on the field is NY and can recite a few players' name, but some of those players haven't been on the team in years.

Attire

They change their Yankee memorabilia as often as they changed their scowl. (So never, really. Their 1996 World Champion Yankee T-shirt is starting to fade.)

How to Talk to Them

Look them right in the eyes when you talk to them. Play the numbers game with them. Since they are usually solitary, confront them with another person or two, or an entire kickboxing team full of anti-Yankee fans.

Slugger Rating 　　　　　　　Use 3x daily.

CIGGAS

Overview

These are middle-aged, cigarette-addicted, smoky-voiced women no one wants to be around. Look at 'em. It's like there's a tiny oxygen tank inside each nicotine stick that they are desperately trying to suck dry. They smoke so many cigarettes mainly because they don't always have a bus exhaust pipe handy. Though they've followed the Yankees for decades, Ciggas regard everyone as a "bastard," even the homely female ushers.

Distinguishing Characteristics

They smell of a garbage dump in Newark and look as if their face was left in the dryer too long. Alligators envy them because Ciggas look so leathery. They're alone and nothing fazes them except perhaps holy water and mouthwash. With a little alcohol, they start to sway and whatever coherence they had ends up as an attempt to meld several languages . . . badly. Therefore, they usually skip right over a "little" alcohol, opting instead to start with a "lot" of alcohol.

Psychology

They have nothing else besides their beloved Yankees and their Winston Salem's. And they love their Yankees, boy. You can tell because they can't finish a rousing cheer without wheezing up an epic chunk of phlegm that looks like Steve Balboni. It is rumored that the bigger the chunk of phlegm, the bigger the Yankee fan.

Background

If you end up sitting next to one of them at a game, you'll have to check yourself into detox just by association. They didn't successfully finish their AA program because the meetings conflicted with televised spring training games. Besides, alcohol gives them the courage to make fools of themselves at games and think they'd legitimately have a shot with Jason Giambi.

How to Talk to Them

They hate you and your team and if you listened to what they yelled at the Yankees, you'd swear they hate them too. They raised their kids with tough love and phrases like, "That's the best you can do? A one-armed ape can draw better than you." Win them over with street-wise terms of endearment such as "Who's your grandson?" and "You my cigga!"

Slugger Rating Okay, we know it should be more, but they've already been beaten down by life.

ALTA CACAS

Overview

A Yiddish term meaning "persnickety old fart," these are the "elder statesmen" of Yankee fans and are the most seasoned and stubborn debaters of all species. Most of them were involved in the original Williams vs. DiMaggio debate. Some even recall first-hand when the Dead Sea was merely "sick." And they all watched their empire crumble to the upstart rebellion in 2004 after years of just blowing them off, chuckling at their ineptitude. It turned their whole world upside-down. All that's left are faded memories of greatness in an era of innocence. Their stories are entertaining, mainly because of their "revisionist" version of history.

Attire

Though the contemporary visor is a sharper style for them, painters caps are still in vogue. Also look for spring jackets circa 1970s.

Where Can You Find Them?

Mostly they are seen at the Yankees spring training facility in and around Tampa, Florida. In fact, the Sunshine State's entire southern hemisphere is the natural habitat to gaggles of them during the winter months.

Changes from the Old Days

Tailgating parties with meats and beer have been replaced with a cooler filled with fruit, bran muffins, and a fast-acting diuretic. A highlight is watching them dance to "Cotton-Eyed Joe."

How to Talk to Them

It's a sort of "Legends Game" for old-time hecklers. They've seen it all and have nothing to prove. Sly comments like, "Reminds me of when the Yankees beat your team in '65" take the place of "Come back and talk to me when you have twenty-six championships," even though you know that's what they're really thinking.

Don't even attempt an argument with them. Imagine having one point-of-view that's been cultivated for centuries and you've got the *Alta Caca*. The roots of their beliefs are so solid that there's no way they'll be able to converse logically with you. While they are rigid in their thinking, they're usually harmless and you have to laugh . . . as they get implanted on your front grill as you run them over. There are moments when they acquiesce to wishing you the best of luck, but even they don't believe that totally.

Slugger Rating Just remember to do it before 4:30p.m. otherwise you'll interrupt their Early Bird dinner special.

ELK

Overview

ELK, or Elderly Loud Knitters, don't actually knit. Any sharp objects like a knitting needle have to be checked at the gate. Are you kidding, in Yankee Stadium? Can you imagine what would happen if they weren't?

These demure ladies of age employ their decades worth of swearing to impress even the raunchiest fan. They are sweet for 90 percent, maybe 91.7 percent of the time. Similar to *Alta Cacas*, it's their world and you won't be able to tell them differently.

Hobbies

Needlepoint, macramé, putting sweaters on lap dogs, singing in the church choir, gardening.

Characteristics Early in the Game

They're quick to scold you for upsetting the peace and decorum in "the Stadium" with your "filthy, potty-mouth language."

Characteristics Late in the Game

As the game goes on, the shots of brandy they've secretly sucked down figure in as they get snookered. Now they're warmed up and it's all coming out; racism and ethnic slurs abound. But they claim, "In my time, that was perfectly and rightfully acceptable." And if you call them on it, ELK won't hesitate to turn on you. "Keep your opinions to yourself, you big-nosed wop."

They usually attend games with a much-younger relative on his prison's "Accompanied Weekend Furlough" program. And they'll need him if they plan on making it out of the stadium without getting bum-rushed by an angry mob of *Jersey Mallrats* and their *Friggin' Utes.*

Baseball Q Rating

They actually know a lot about stats and such, but refuse to get into barroom-type hypotheticals. Some keep score during the game, throwing it out if the Yankees lose so they can look back years later on the Yankees "perfect season." In scorekeeping, they invented the abbreviation "UB" in place of "E" for "<u>U</u>mpire <u>B</u>lew the call thus giving the other team an advantage."

How to Talk to Them

Avoid talking to them about baseball at all costs, unless, of course, you desire a crochet needle lodged in your retina. Instead, shower them with nostalgic references to their generation. "Ma'am, you've sure got a lot of moxie. You remind me of a young and more attractive Rosie the Riveter."

Slugger Rating

Zero bats, as you will be looked down upon if you lay or even *think* about laying a finger on her. Plus, she'll go down faster than Patrick Ewing in the paint.

YANKEE FANS INTERNATIONAL (A.K.A. THE MATSUIMEN)

Overview

They are fervent Yankee fans by way of Matsui or any other Asian-born player that represents his nation on the Yankees. Put it this way, if Matsui were an Atlanta Brave, they'd start a Tomahawk chop. If Matsui were a Chicago Cub, they'd roast a Billy goat. If Matsui were a pig farmer in Alabama, they'd relentlessly chant, "Mat-Sooeey!"

The Matsuimen are the most abundant of the foreign fans at the stadium. They fill entire sections eagerly waiting for Matsui to hit a dinger, yet have no idea what a "dinger" is. Even though the Matsuimen allegiance is not to the team, they are smart enough to root for the Yankees because if they do well then they'll know that Matsui is happy. (Popular misconception: In order to save face, they commit mass Hari-kari if Matsui goes zero-for-whatever or grounds into a double play with the bases loaded.)

Psychology

It's been a long time coming that a major Japanese star takes over America's pastime on U.S. soil. The Americans who've played in Japan were only reserve ballplayers. So far, only Ichiro (a.k.a. The Artist Formerly Known as Suzuki) has been good enough to shed his last name. Unfortunately, "Hideki" only serves to connote the image of the "fat toad" Irabu.

Physiology

They are always Asian. Though many Latin American players make it to the majors, their fans root for the entire team and not just their fellow countrymen.

Attire

Cloaked head-to-toe in one-size-too-big Yankees gear, with the brim of their hat flatter than a Kevin Brown curve ball. Cameras always at the ready to capture Matsui's at-bat, Matsui in the field, Matsui smoking a cigarette in the dugout . . .

How to Talk to Them

There's not much call to talk to them as they mostly travel in packs, preferring to remain immersed in their own culture. If you feel the need to start a conversation with them, here's a list of helpful phrases to *avoid*:

- So, what do you think of the Yanks' middle relief this year?

- Matsui? Is that Japanese for "crater face?"
- I bet you guys really "love Matsui long-time!"
- Matsui hit a bigger bomb than Nagasaki.
- Anything in English.

Hobbies

Photographing everything, singing Karaoke, and listening to Sinatra's "New York, New York."

Gabby Cabbies

A subset of the Matsuimen, G.C.s are only "fans" to relate to their customers. The New York Yankees are simply used as conversation fodder along with the best routes to use to get to LaGuardia, how to get camel hair out of your birkah, and how the United States is the greatest country in the world. Also, they supply deep advice on matters of the heart. They're recognizable by the yellow boat on wheels that they wrap around themselves.

You should prepare yourself for a barrage of these archetypal phrases that they're sure to drop on you with relative ease:

- "I am praying for this Bernie Williams to hit a touchdown."
- "My favorite Yankee is that Cotton-Eyed Joe."
- "Great hot dog but needs humus."

Slugger rating Sadly, the Geneva Convention prohibits us from issuing any more beatings.

OPEN–MINDED, KNOWLEDGEABLE YANKEE FANS

His name is Mike Drinan. He lives in Poughkeepsie.

How to Talk to Them

Email yankeefan1@greatestyankeefanever.com

Slugger Rating Just to keep him open-minded.

THE POPULATION BREAKS DOWN AS SUCH

- Most likely to spit popcorn: Jersey Mallrats, Friggin' Utes, Out-of-Townies
- Most likely to curse using words you've never heard before: Friggin' Utes, ELK, Alta Cacas, Mafioso Meatballs
- Most likely to stop following them during a period out of first place: Alta Cacas, Out-of-Townies, Bandwagon Biyatches, Gabby Cabbies
- Most likely to have served time: Mafioso Meatballs, Ciggas, Jersey Mallrats
- Most likely to start a fight: Jeckyls, Out-of-Townies, Jersey Mallrats
- Most likely to end a fight: Mafioso Meatballs
- Most likely to think Roger Clemens is still on the team: Out-of-Townies, Geckos
- Most likely to not know Clemens was *ever* on the team: Bandwagon Bi-yatches, Geckos, Matsuimen, Friggin' Utes
- Most able to have a decent conversation with   Mike Drinan: Tearjerker Jerks
- Most likely to get kicked out of a game: Jersey Mallrats, Jeckyls
- Most likely to have nothing else going for them in their life besides the Yankees: Ciggas, Tearjerker Jerks
- Most likely to read this book: Mike Drinan

There you have the minutiae about Yankee fans. Scary, isn't it, how many types there actually are. Such subtle differences in what is fundamentally the same genetic pool. Ask most people to describe Yankee fans and they'll say there are two types: arrogant Yankee fans and REALLY arrogant Yankee fans.

The next time you're at "the Stadium," play a game with your companions. See who can pick out the most types accurately. For each one you see, give yourself TWO POINTS. Add ONE POINT each time they do something listed in their description. For example, if you spot an ELK unleashing an ethnic slur, that's a P.A.T. for you.

Have fun!

CHAPTER THREE—
THE BIGGEST FAN OF ALL

Like any loyal subject, Yankee fans pattern themselves after their leader and the Number One Yankee Fan in the world, the one who puts them together and tears them apart; the one who wants to win so much that he's willing to financially obliterate all competitors—King George Steinbrenner. The traits present in themselves, they acquire by watching and emulating Him—his arrogance, his brash nature, his impulsive streak, his corruption, his indifference toward baseball itself, etc. Who is this man they call George? How did he become the wealthiest owner in sports and build his Evil Empire?

> I look at Steinbrenner as a kind of later day Howard Hughes character: impulsive, loaded with cash and stark raving mad.
>
> — *Matt Kennedy*

STEINBRENNER: THE UNAUTHORIZED BIOGRAPHY*

George Michael Steinbrenner III was born on Independence Day in 1930. Known best as the principal owner of the New York Yankees, he is also known as "the Boss," "the guy who ruined baseball," "Steinfuhror," "Darth Steinbrenner," "cocksucker," and "Tiny" to his friends at the golf club.

Born in Rocky River, Ohio, young Georgie grew up in a suburb of Cleveland during the Great Depression. During those lean years, he was forced to sell apples off a cart to help his family make ends meet. But other vendors complained when Georgie would steal the best apples off of their carts and put them with his own.

*Number of sources used in research (0)

Known as a shrewd kickball captain in grade school, he always found the best players by giving them more cookies than the other captains. His teams set records for best offensive production for a team and consecutive wins (42). Most of the fourth graders on his team were later found out to be between twelve and fourteen years old, thus requiring an asterisk by their records.

As a young man, he matriculated at Williams College where he ran track while majoring in Business Ethics until he flunked out. Given another chance, George changed his major to sports management. After flunking again he settled on poetry; coming in third in his fraternity's annual dirty Limerick contest.

GEORGE'S THIRD-PLACE LIMERICK

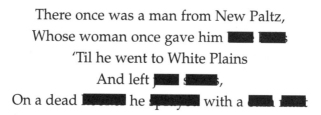

There once was a man from New Paltz,
Whose woman once gave him ▰▰ ▰▰;
'Til he went to White Plains
And left ▰▰ ▰▰,
On a dead ▰▰▰ he ▰▰▰ with a ▰▰ ▰▰

After graduation, he joined the United States Air Force and became the first enlisted man to put an offer into the government to buy the Air Force, thereby forcing the government to discharge him dishonorably, burn his records, and disavow any knowledge of his ever participating in the armed forces.

He returned to his home state where he coached high school basketball and football in Columbus before becoming an assistant football coach at Northwestern University. He was relieved of his coaching duties after one morning when he got into a disagreement with the head coach and fired him. When the athletic director informed Coach Steinbrenner that he did not have the authority to fire other coaches, George fired him too.

Deciding it best that he focus more on a family at that point, George married Joan Zieg, in a small civil ceremony in 1956. They divorced in 1958, remarried in 1959, divorced again six months later, remarried, divorced again the following spring, and then remarried. The third marriage was not recognized however as he failed to realize that she was married to someone else at the time. They have been married now for forty-five years consecutively.

With his wife locked up in a long-term deal, he went back to work, this time joining his father's struggling shipbuilding business, the American Shipbuilding Company, a year later.

Stealing some money from his daughter's Girl Scout troop's hedge fund they kept for a trip to Disney World, George bought the Cleveland Pipers of the National Industrial Basketball League. The team went bankrupt and he went back to the shipbuilding company, eventually buying it.

After failing in his bid to buy the Cleveland Indians (whom he continually referred to as the "Cleveland Prairie Savages"), he joined a group of investors to buy the Yankees for $10 million in 1973.

After announcing at his press conference, "I won't be active in the day-to-day operations of the club at all," he changed his tune quickly. In his first year as owner, he ordered the carpet pattern changed in his office a record sixteen times, prompting the facilities department and maintenance staff to go on strike for two months in mid-July.

During games, he would routinely pull vendors aside and criticize their selling technique. This prompted the Concessionaires Union to fine him $20,000 and ban him from the concession stands during games.

At this time, free agency was becoming popular in the major leagues. It proved to be a boon for Steinbrenner for in 1974, he bought Catfish Hunter, then he bought Richard Nixon, then, during a particularly wet spell that summer, he bought the weatherman and ordered him to stop the rain. That latter maneuver got both him and the weatherman suspended for two years.

Upon return from his suspension, his team won the first of six World Championships under his reign. But the fans' arrogance and their growing familiarization with winning began to show after losing the ALCS in 1980 and the World Series in 1981, as they became disenchanted with his ownership. After Game Five that year, George got into a scuffle with two fans in an elevator that left him with a broken hand, a fat lip, and a bruised goiter. The fans, Mildred Schuster, ninety-three, and Catherine Dinovio, eighty-nine, were unscathed in the scuffle.

Continuing with his random day-to-day decisions, the team saw a steady stream of stars flee from what had now been tabbed "the Bronx Zoo." Hall-of-Fame outfielder, Dave Winfield, was one of the few who turned down a trade away from New York to the Mighty California Angels of Los Angeles in Orange County's Anaheim in exchange for pitcher Mike Witt in May of 1990. Steinbrenner rewarded Winfield's loyalty by refusing to pay his charity foundation the $300,000 guaranteed in his contract, then trading him anyway.

Later that year, Steinbrenner confessed to also paying Howard Spira, a small-time gambler, $40,000 to dig up dirt on Winfield. This was the final straw for baseball (and for Winfield who claimed he was worth way more than $40,000). Commissioner Fay Vincent suspended Steinbrenner for life. Evidently, Vincent, a huge animal lover, meant the *life* of his pet hamster, DiMaggio, and reinstated Steinbrenner three years later.

Since then, Steinbrenner put his business savvy to work purchasing a new cable station (YES Network), four new championships, and is in on-going talks to build a new stadium outside of the Bronx.

And shortly after New York blew the three-game lead over nemesis Boston in the ALCS, "the Stein" went out and purchased fireballers Randy Johnson and Carl Pavano, as well as all present and future residents of Cuba, Puerto Rico, and the island of Okinawa. He is also rumored to have put the Dominican Republic on layaway.

Currently, Mr. Steinbrenner can be heard regularly cursing and randomly firing people on the streets of New York. Homeless people won't go near him because they say he's too senile, cheap, and reeks of formaldehyde.

Now that we know about Steinbrenner's life, let's let bygones be bygones and have a friendly game of kickball. We drew together a diverse sample of people to participate in the exercise. We then went to MENSA and recruited the world's foremost psychologists, theologists, microbiologists, and lots of other "-ologists." Unfortunately, we couldn't find a park that would let us play nor could we get everyone's schedule clear at the same time. So instead we set up a think tank in a makeshift airport hangar, ordered dim sum, and asked them this following question:

"YOU'RE THE CAPTAIN OF YOUR KICKBALL TEAM, WHO WOULD YOU PICK LAST—JUDAS, OSAMA BIN LADEN, OR GEORGE STEINBRENNER?"

Using different reasoning and fighting between choosing with their heart or with their head, our group came to several vastly different conclusions.

There are people who would be proud to have George Steinbrenner on their team. Dustin Millman, YES Network employee, would jump at the chance of picking his boss. And wisely so as he feels Steinbrenner would then buy other players for him.

Raj Nath simply wants him on his team so he can make fun of him every time he muffs a ball. Comedian Paul Nardizzi would also select Georgie without the slightest hesitation to give him a piece of his mind.

Vermont resident, Ray Lambert is thinking big. "I'd pick Steinbrenner first and then use him AS the kickball so both teams could kick the crap out of him." Ray would make a great big league manager some day with that mindset. However, his son, Sean Lambert, takes a more diplomatic stance. "Judas hung himself, so at least he felt a sense of remorse. The U.S. government still can't locate Bin Laden, so he might use those same elusive skills on the base paths. I'm certain Steinbrenner will always be a spoiled, insane, deceptive, snake oil salesman who will forever plot and scheme his way above his station and be the last one I would pick for my kickball team."

Matt Kennedy, noted Yankee fan-puncher, on the other hand, quickly jumps on the Osama Bin Laden bandwagon, impressed with the man's dedication. "At least he believes in something. But Steinbrenner, alternatively, would be my last pick because he's an over privileged rich boy with a sense of entitlement and fake rage that gets represented as passion. Besides, he's a blow hard with almost no actual baseball knowledge, and I believe he's a felon as well."

Some refused to make a pick before looking at the reports from each player's private physician. There's the question over who's in the worst shape. Adam Sivits believes Bin Laden is old and spindly and remembers from our unauthorized bio that Steinbrenner was an athlete. Benjamin Hill is more familiar with Bin Laden's kidney problems and so he'd pick the terrorist last for no other reason than dragging a dialysis machine around the base paths doesn't make you a threat to steal.

However, Angelica Fisichella guesses that Steinbrenner is in the worst physical shape and would pick OBL before the Yankees owner.

The most religious member of the bunch, Keith Camire, a devout Christian would unequivocally select Judas last, without a doubt.

Well, that is, unless Jesus wasn't watching, and then he'd pick Steinbrenner last.

BJ Cook, prison guard, doesn't want to get into health status, religious affiliation, or base-running ability, all he knows is he would sooner play a man short than pick Steinbrenner.

But let's not forget that we've mentioned three evil men here. If you're picking your team, don't you think that past transgressions would be part of the criteria you used? Fifteen-year-old Braves fan Davy Marsh considered his choices and came to the conclusion that being American, he hates Bin Laden, but he identifies more with hating Yankees, and hence would choose the FBI's Most-Wanted Man ahead of Baseball's Most-Hated Man.

FUN FACT:

Four thousand Yankee fans polled were asked what the capital of New York is. Eighty-nine (or more than 4 percent) said the capital of New York was George Steinbrenner.

If you're looking for a measurement to identify the most offensive of these three men, feel free to use the "Billy Abelson scale of evil." He would choose Bin Laden last, whom he deems much more evil than Steinbrenner and a little less evil than Darth Vader. (Check his website to find out *"Quien es mas macho?"*)

Chris Lopez and Ken Moore went further with this and put their baseball feelings aside realizing that although Steinbrenner is a dipstick, he has never been a part of killing anybody. Hence, they'd also pick Bin Laden last. Before you jump down their throats, it doesn't mean they'd give Steinbrenner playing time.

Jimmy Dunn, stand-up comedian and former host of NESN's *Fan Attic*, is an out-of-the-box thinker who'd pick Steinbrenner first for more selfish reasons: "We'd be the only kickball team with our own private jet!"

CHAPTER FOUR—
THE BAD, THE WORSE AND THE UGLY

A trip to the jungle: Yankee Stadium. Located in the heart of the Bronx (as everyone knows, "Bronx" is a Dutch word meaning "Your horse has shat on my foot"), it is considered one of the most historic parks in major league baseball, if not the most legendary. Having opened on April 18, 1923, it's frequently referred to as the "House that Ruth Built." But that noble title has been supplanted more recently by the nickname, the Bronx Zoo.

To many visitors, it's more like a prison or insane asylum where the inmates roam free amongst the unsuspecting public. One of the more frequently asked questions at the *How to Talk to a Yankee Fan Institute* is what can be done to deal with Yankee fans *in* Yankee Stadium.

> Everyone there is mean, drunk, loud, rude, nasty, and miserable. They're negative and violent. Even the women look and act like hardened criminals.
>
> — *Laurie Russo, Queens, NY*

> Yankee Stadium is the place to go if you want your car stolen, or to get beaten up when they have mini-bat give-away night.
>
> — *Greg Faherty*

But hey, if you don't believe them, why not buy a ticket for Yankee Stadium yourself? Just be careful. The fans are like gremlins: do not taunt them, do not get them drunk, and, whatever you do— do NOT turn your back on them! The following incidents have actually happened and, most likely, will happen again. May God be with you.

> **FUN FACT:**
> *If you take all the crack whores in the Yankee Stadium parkinglot and stretch them end-to-end, they would be able to reach the midway point of the George Washington Bridge.*

Why does this Institute concern itself more with the grounds of baseball than the fans? There was a recent article in the Institute's signature journal, *Yankee Fan Quarterly*, highlighting problems encountered with the fans in a public arena where various fans co-mingled. Their study showed that the probability of a violent rendezvous with a Yankee fan increases five-fold at Yankee Stadium. (It increases by almost seven-fold after they stop serving beer.)

Throughout this chapter, we'll borrow anecdotes from the journal as reference material for our studies. (FYI, as insightful and thought provoking as *Yankee Fan Quarterly* is, we do not recommend picking up their annual swimsuit edition. Think Mama Leone in a Speedo. Yeech!)

IT'S RAINING FOOD AND DRINK

> I actually went to Yankee Stadium to watch them play Cleveland (I got free tickets) and decided to wear my B hat. Some jackass stole it and threw a beer at me.
> — *Mikhael Krzymnacker*

> One time in Yankee Stadium in the mid-'90s, a friend from Texas was rooting for the Rangers and some of the surrounding New Yorkers began throwing popcorn and ice at him. I never saw that happen in any other park I went to!
> — *Dave Wyckoff, Nashville, TN*

We'd learned of this earlier from Dr. Hoffenhoffen. First off, be thankful they're not throwing feces like some of their evolutionary ancestors. Secondly, take this lesson with you—talking to any fan whose arm is cocked back like Mariano Rivera is pretty much impossible. They've made up their mind. Besides, at that point, the only thing you should be thinking of is ducking.

SOMEONE CALL THE POLICE . . . THEN GET HELP!

No one is safe at "the Zoo." Not even top brass. Boston Red Sox co-owner Tom Werner went to Yankee Stadium during the 1998 World Series when he was the owner of the Padres. His account, printed in the *Boston Globe* in October of 2004, is as follows:

I went to the concession stand behind home plate with my son. I was wearing a Padres hat. A Yankee fan came up to me and said, "Take off your hat." I said, "Why?" He cursed at me. I walked away. He came after me and said, "Did you hear me?" I said, "Yes, I heard you." So he pushed me. There was a cop ten feet away. I said, "Don't push me." He cursed at me again. I asked the cop, "Why don't you do anything?" And the cop said, "You're lucky he didn't slug you."

Perhaps this is an anomaly. We defer to Clyde Haberman of the *New York Times* for his examination and assessment of the Bronx fans.

Despite a longstanding ban on smoking, fans lit up defiantly. One such smoker, a potty-mouthed yo-yo, was led away by security guards, only to return an inning later. "They don't eject you when you're a cop," he said. (*NY Times* 10/11/05)

There's a reason *CSI: NY* did an episode where a Red Sox fan was being harassed in Yankee Stadium. (Original airdate: 5/11/05) Can you say, "art imitating life"? If anything, that teaches one not to expect to be saved by a knight in a shiny blue uniform either. You take your own well-being in your hands as well as risk life, liberty, and the pursuit of happiness when you attend a game in the Bronx and don't root for the home team.

Mr. Werner was correct to implore the cop to assist him. On-duty police officers are more likely NOT to punish you for your allegiances. He may not help you, but standing around him can't hurt as much as standing in another part of the concourse with a hot dog shoved up your nose, courtesy of a "spirited" Yankee fan.

But if you're going to talk to Mr. Policeman, try to keep your fandom nebulous. "I'm not really a huge fan" and "my wife dragged me here and made me wear this silly Orioles T-shirt" are good phrases to use. In the event a fan hurts you, the cop will be more inclined to testify for you in the name of his sworn duty if he thinks you weren't there rooting against his team.

FUN FACT:

In 1999, Yankee fans swiped over 15,000 items from fans of other teams including hats, souvenir balls, signed scorecards, ice cream sandwiches, and a toddler's pacifier.

RATED "F.U." FOR BAD LANGUAGE

> When I was seven, I went to a Yankees-Braves game in the first year of interleague play. Some lady started to curse at me because I was wearing a Braves hat until I started to cry. It was awful.
>
> — *Davy Marsh, 15, NYC*

We assume he's using the term "lady" loosely. If you think it's not a place for children, just listen to what the children themselves are saying.

> At one game, we sat in the bleachers when this six-year-old kid with his parents turns to my friend (wearing his Twins jersey) and says, "You're a fuckin' asshole." When dealing with normal people, you would expect the parents to

scold the kid or at the very least apologize to my friend for their kid's behavior. But we are dealing with a Yankee fan. Instead, the parent turns around, laughing, and says, "Ha ha. He just called you a fuckin' asshole."

— *AV, Met fan*

AV is obviously a very patient man, but we're guessing that Yankee Stadium is no longer high on his list of Saturday afternoon hangouts.

Most Yankee fans are proud of their reputation. They wear it as a badge of malice. Blues musician, Jim Chilson, had a recent run-in with Yankee fans at a Sox/Yanks game in the Bronx that provides support to these claims. "When leaving the stadium, after the Sox won . . . a bunch of Yankee fans yelled to us, 'Boston Sucks!' A girl with us said, 'Oh, that's classy!' One of the guys shot back, 'Hey, if you want class than why don't you just go back to Boston?' . . . I think that says it all."—All aboard the Class Express. Next stop, Beantown!

ESSENTIAL EQUIPMENT FOR ANY FAN TO ATTEND A GAME IN YANKEE STADIUM

1. **Rain-slicker:** to shield self from beer-throwers and spitters
2. **Batting helmet:** protects head from heavy objects that could cause brain damage and make you act like the animals around you
3. **GPS antenna (in helmet):** to locate your body
4. **Dark sunglasses:** to cut the glare off of pasty NYC dwellers dancing to "Cotton Eyed Joe"
5. **"Groucho Marx" fake nose and moustache disguise:** conceals identity to protect family from repercussions
6. **Ear-plugs:** to block out constant taunting in annoying *New Yawwwk* accent
7. **Flak vest:** added protection for walk to car or ride on NYC subway
8. **Belt:** to hang self if your team blows another one

9. **Protective cup:** shields the family jewels to insure ability to breed future Yankee-haters
10. **Boxing glove:** for fighting back
11. **Cell phone:** to call 9-1-1
12. **AM-FM radio:** to listen to play-by-play from your home sports radio announcers whose vocal chords you don't want to rip out
13. **Goalie's blocker pad:** to deflect incoming food
14. **Biker's wallet attached by chain:** for obvious reasons
15. **Steel-toed boots:** to clear a path when leaving the stadium

16. **Shin-pads:** protects legs from derelict children of Yankees fans who are told, "Kick him!"
17. **Yankees Suck! t-shirt (under flak-vest):** just because

You might deem it impossible to speak with Yankee fans when their language is so barbaric. But that's just when you know you got 'em where you want 'em. Should you encounter a *Friggin' Ute* or a *Cigga* or a "potty-mouthed yo yo" as Haberman describes, simply talk to them in their own language.

Escaping Yankee Stadium can be the best option to avoiding them and, therefore, the best way to converse with them, but many times Yankee fans follow you to your park and make themselves right at home. Their favorite homes away from home are Shea Stadium and Fenway *Pahk.*

One particularly poignant journalistic piece in *YF Quarterly* exposed the dangers in your own park from migrating Yankee fans that seem to invade by the truckload.

COMING TO A STADIUM NEAR YOU

> Sitting in the bleachers at Fenway during a Yanks game, we argued back and forth with a bunch of pinstripe-wearing a-holes who threw a beer at us. (How stupid—a real fan would NEVER waste a beer like that!) We ended up missing half the game because they were so obnoxious. The Sox won and the pinheads were tossed out in the seventh proving that "good" can prevail over "evil."
>
> — *Kate DiStefano*

Not that Sox fans are complete angels in all of this. In the interest of a partisan rebuttal, let's listen to a Yankee fan's take on the subject:

So chanting "Yankees suck!" on Opening Day versus Tampa Bay before the opening pitch makes Red Sox Nation better fans? When I bring my five-year-old son to your venerable old park and he hears this for the first time, he asks, "Daddy, why are they saying that bad word?"

— *Layne Koss*

Thank you for helping us to make a point. It's while at other stadiums that they take their blinders off and notice things after ignoring them at home—Yankee Stadium, the foul-mouthed capital of the world. The biased Yankee fan does not see the huge ratio of bad incidents at their park compared to the same occurrence at others.

For every Layne Koss story, there are a dozen Matt Kennedy stories, (NOTE: "a dozen" is only a rough estimate as the actual number ranges anywhere from 2—400,000) where some members of society emulate Peter Finch's "Howard Beale" of the movie *Network*—they're "mad as hell and they're not gonna take it anymore!"

In 1994, I attended a Sox game in the Bronx. I was sitting with my #42 Mo Vaughn jersey on. When big Mo hit a dinger, I did a homer dance in the aisle and I was pelted with various things, cups, napkins, etc . . . It was all in good fun until some chucklehead decided to throw a pretzel full of mustard at me. Something made my head turn seconds before impact and it caught me square in the face. I took exception, scaled a couple of steps and punched him in his stupid face six or seven times until he bled profusely. Ah, to be young.

— *Matt Kennedy, Wood-Ridge, NJ*

Matt chose to let his fists do the talking. While that goes against everything we stand for, we understand what was going through his head . . . it was a pretzel full of mustard. Next time, Matt, before avenging the pretzel, just for kicks, yell "I'm mad as hell, and I'm not gonna take it anymore."

This is one of those rare times when the thrower ends up being pummeled by the throwee. Punks, chuckleheads, and lowlifes—a day at the ballpark has never been so fun. So if you would rather skip the physical and mental intimidation and decide to watch the game elsewhere, just know that even outside those hallowed baseball grounds, they're lurking in the shadows—the classless Yankee fan.

FUN FACT:

Sean Milton of Hoboken holds the record for number of popcorn kernels spit into the hair of opposing fans during a nine-inning game. On Sunday, May 16, 2002, he spit 398 kernels at various stadium-goers. Never satisfied with greatness, Sean returned the next night intent on smashing his new career mark, but was beaten senseless by a number of Baltimore fans after only forty-six kernels were discharged.

FIVE–STAR LOWLIFES

During the 2004 ALCS, I dined in the restaurant of a five-star inn and retired to the lounge where I could watch the game. Two couples, all handsomely dressed, came in to take their desserts. Upon hearing that I was a Sox fan, they asked me to leave. One woman said, "How could anyone root for the Sox? They are disgusting, they look like hoodlums, their hair is sloppy . . . they are just so un-American." I asked what, exactly, an American looks like? No one responded immediately and then the woman said, "Look at how awful their uniforms are. The team is a mess. They should all get haircuts. They look like drug addicts. They need to set an example for everyone." I said, "But they are wonderful ballplayers and it's all about the competition. They set an example by virtue of how well and fair they play the game." All four grimaced while eyeing me with contempt. For the next hour, they continued a barrage of distasteful comments. I tried to watch the game, but their continuing ill manners robbed me of my joy. So I chose to leave.

— *Elise Lee, writer*

Oh . . . so we guess guys like Hideki Matsui, Mariano Rivera, and Jorge Posada are more "American" than those Red Sox players. Perhaps Jason Varitek, Trot Nixon, and Tim Wakefield better work on getting that Green Card and visa.

Did Ms. Lee do the right thing? Leaving is always one way to go. Yankee fans are looking to ruin any dissenting fan's leisure time. You can be the better fan and know that you're a class higher than them. Or you can pour wine on them before leaving making you feel good, but bringing yourself down to their level.

You could send them a plate of crackers, and when they ask why, you can reply that you thought crackers would go nicely with their *whine*. [Rim shot] But they might not get it and you've lost out on stunning them with a zinger.

Why not approach them with diplomacy? In Chapter Ten, we'll explore that avenue, but here, these people are not connected to you in any way; you owe them no courtesy and hence can only talk to them as they do to you—with a holier-than-thou attitude.

But going out on top, yes, Elise did the right thing. The moral for her, she said, was "that you can dine in a five-star inn, but you can not necessarily expect to find five-star people, no matter how financially set they might be." A-ha! A moral! We knew it was here somewhere. Looking at Chapter Two, how many bats do you think they should receive? In keeping with the theme of this passage, we here at *HTTTYF* suggest five . . . apiece, naturally.

HELLO . . . IS THIS GAME ON?!

Run-ins like Ms. Lee's can happen anywhere, when you're not expecting it. There doesn't even have to be a game going on. Red Sox fan Chris Lopez went to the movies wearing his Manny cap and "Big Papi" shirt. When he went to the concession stand, the cashier revealed herself to be a Yankee fan, saying, "I don't really feel like selling this to you with that crap you're wearing." After some arguing and the threat of calling her supervisor over, she finally gave him his order, almost "forgetting" to include his change as well.

Yankee fans put any semblance of professionalism aside to promote the rivalry between them and other fans. As much as they'd like to think withholding someone's snacks is justified, they're in no position to show bias.

Take, for instance, this tale that took place on December 24, 2004, a short two months after the Yanks' hated rivals defeated them in the ALCS and went on to win the World Series four games to none against the St. Louis Cardinals. Red Sox fan Mike Sheehan was in Los Angeles buying a copy of Stephen King's *Faithful*. He relayed this to us:

> When the cashier scanned the item for purchase, he chuckled under his breath, "Enjoy it while you can. It was a fluke."
>
> I shot back, "Hate us all you want, but it's hard to call eight post-season wins in a row a fluke. Now you have a small taste of what we go through every year with you guys."
>
> The cashier puffed out his chest and locked eyes with me, barking, "Yeah, and what are you going to do about it?"
>
> I laughed, "Me *personally* or the Red Sox?"

A million thoughts raced through his head. I could almost smell brain matter sizzling. "Yeah? Whydoncha' come back and talk to me when you have twenty-six World Series titles!"

"I will. And I suspect you'll still be working the counter here at the bookstore. Merry Christmas."

And those are the stories that don't get publicized (except in *YF Quarterly*). There are other more famous anecdotes that have accumulated over the years simply adding to the "legacy" of Yankee fans. Have you ever heard about a switchblade being thrown at Wally Joyner in another park? Not bloody likely! But in the "Zoo" . . .

> Joyner escaped injury when he was grazed on the arm by a knife thrown from the stands after the game as he talked with [pitcher Mike] Witt. "We were heading toward the dugout and I felt this thing brush my arm," Joyner said. It didn't cut me or anything so I thought it was a comb or something somebody threw from the second row. Then I looked down, and it was this big Bowie knife. The thing had about a five-inch blade on it. (*NY Times*, 8/27/86)

How many times has a hat been stolen off a Yankee player's head during a game? But an opposing player in Ruth's House . . .

> During an 11-6 loss to the Yankees at the Stadium, the Boston Red Sox rushed into the stands in the eighth inning to retrieve a hat stolen from leftfielder Jim Rice after a play in the outfield in which he collided with shortstop Spike Owen. Two fans received summons, the one who took the hat, and the one who wrestled with Rice in the stands. And as the Sox were in the stands,

someone else snatched pitcher Dennis Boyd's hat. (*NY Times*, 9/14/86)

And this was a mere two weeks after the Joyner incident! (We presume security hadn't yet received the memo.) Again, security there has a lot on their plate. They're a little outnumbered so they can't always treat each incident with the care and commitment needed. But we'll give them the benefit of the doubt and say they are doing the best they can to protect the visitors and their fans as soundly as they would their own team.

Ask yourself how many fans jump into the protective screen behind home plate at Wrigley or the Jake? We'd make a guess there are a few more instances of that in the Bronx.

Sure, many teams have bad seeds. Okay, so Yankee fans now have the name Chris House to pull out of their distorted memory bank. For those who don't remember, House was the guy who, while allegedly going for the ball during a mid-April 2005 game at Fenway, let his hands get too close to Sheffield and accidentally bumped his face. The event was blown way out of proportion. Due to the aftermath of the situation, Dave O'Connor was moved to write the following editorial to the *Boston Globe*:

> To the Yankees and members of the press,
>
> Chris House is no doubt nothing more than a drunken hothead who doesn't deserve to be in the presence of the team he's supported his whole life, right? I've studied the footage carefully, the same footage that all media outlets had at their disposal and to be honest, I don't see where House was even *looking* at Sheffield, and I certainly don't see where House's hand (open, not in a fist) comes even close to Sheffield's face. But immediately, the gang from ESPN says House is a punk while Sheffield showed "great restraint." MSNBC's *Countdown with Keith*

Olbermann found a way to equate the incident with the on-field beating death of a Little League player in California.

It has become fashionable lately to call the Yankees a "class" organization to contrast earlier perceptions that the team had no class. Yet Joe Torre and his Yankees feel they know who House is and exactly what was going on in his mind as the ball rolled along the base of the wall. Yankee pitcher Tanyon Sturtze (yes, the same guy who attacked Gabe Kapler from behind during "the melee" in 2004 only to get body slammed to the ground by Big Papi) said, "House was clearly trying to hit Sheffield." Sturtze then went on to say that if it were him, he would have left the field of play and beaten the fan. Nice.

Even Torre, **before** watching the video, diagnosed House as a "threat to society who shouldn't be allowed to walk the streets, much less come to a ballgame." He and Steinbrenner had similar comments about the bullpen worker who was assaulted by two Yankee players during a game in the 2003 ALCS.

Watch the video and be honest about what you see. Chris House is not a thug and he's not an idiot. He's just a fan who messed up.

In five short paragraphs, Dave summed it up skillfully. Yes, it happened on national TV for all to see, but to claim that the Red Sox fans are bigger thugs . . . ? I believe the term is "*Cigga*, puh-lease."

Yankee fans will say that they aren't as big thugs as other fans, even with their reputation. Remember, we're *comparing* here. And given the facts, stories, statistics, etc., there's no way you can accurately or with any sort of sanity claim that any stadium is less safe than Yankee Stadium. We'll grant you that it's hard to see the trees when you're in the forest. But then, how far into the forest are some of these fans?!

After the Ron Artest "incident" in Detroit in November of 2004 where players were suspended, fans were arrested, and the teams, city, and arena officials were embarrassed on national television, New York fan "kizzlecor" hopped on-line to post this message:

> *What a joke!!! Posted by kizzlecor—Nov 20, 2004, 3:06 pm*
> *Where the hell was security? Sleeping? All were wrong, but I don't blame Artest. Anyone would've done the same thing if someone tossed a beer at us. Booze should be banned in Detroit arenas—they obviously don't know how to handle it. Come to NYC and learn how to be a fan!*

Well put. So does this course on "How to Be a Fan" come with an English-to-mongoloid dictionary, giant foam middle finger, and throwing mugs . . . or are those extra?

Obviously, kizzlecor has never been to a game in New York City in his life. But, given what we've seen, who can blame him?

A few months after this posting, in the summer of 2005, yet another fan jumped onto the netting behind home plate in the Bronx prompting White Sox manager Ozzie Guillen to say, "I've never seen anything like that before. I think that's New York, you know, anything can happen." (ESPN.com, August 9, 2005)

During Game Six of the 2004 ALCS police in riot gear had to be summoned onto the field when unruly fans protested the umpires calling Alex Rodriguez out for attempting to knock the ball out of the pitcher's glove on a close play at first, which is a Bush-league play and illegal. I guess the cops were there only because all the good seats were taken in the stands and they wanted to watch the game.

COME TO NEW YORK CITY; LEARN HOW TO BE A REAL FAN!

There's that pesky occipital lobe problem we spoke of in Chapter One. Interesting that Yankee fans could even allow this to ooze from their lips. There were more than thirty arrests in 1999 during the World Series victory parade, the *third* time in four years the Yankees won. People were hit with bottles, newspapers, rolls of toilet paper, and other objects. The arrests ranged from charges of sexual abuse and indecent exposure to inciting a riot and assaulting a police officer. Sexual abuse?! One guy was arrested for groping a woman. We suppose when they say, "learn to be a fan," they mean to ratchet the sexual abuse up a notch. Then we'll be "good" fans.

Let's put aside our differences for one moment and just talk about the "sports celebration." One thing we've always wondered about is how riots break out during these supposedly congratulatory, exuberant occasions. Does someone say to another:

"Hey, man, wanna go see the Yankees?"

"Nah, I'm not in the mood for a game."

"It's not a game. They just won the Series. It's a parade."

"Oh, yeah? Then hang on a sec, I'll go get my explosive projectiles."

This is true after many celebrations, but made popular by NY. (More in a moment!)

Okay, back to the topic at hand. Do Yankee fans not remember those days? Evidently, selective memory has reached epidemic proportions in the boroughs. Even the front office has their horse blinders on. Yankees President Randy Levine commented on the "lawlessness in Boston" after two Yankee players, by most accounts, attacked a groundskeeper in the Sox bullpen during the 2003 ALCS. (*USA Today*, 10/13/03) Sox owner John Henry asked Levine to retract his words, but Levine declined. I guess he believes a groundskeeper taunting his players is a no-no. But when opposing players have hats stolen and knives thrown at them, he adopts a "don't ask, don't tell" strategy. Nice precedent to set for the fans, Randy-boy!

Of course, Levine's familiarity of the history of ballpark lawlessness is a little skewed. Though he wasn't involved with the regime that ran "the Stadium" in the '80s, it's clear he should've at least been briefed on the subject before opening his pie-hole. It gives the illusion that an "eyes shut" policy starts at the top. Or maybe it *is* an illusion? Wait, where was David Copperfield when all this happened? Perhaps he had something to do with it. Conspiracy theorists . . . discuss.

A HISTORY OF VIOLENCE

Noted baseball author Frank DeFord gave a lecture at the 2005 *Los Angeles Times* Festival of Books. Referring to incidents between fans and players, he said incidents like that are "gonna happen periodically," then reminded the crowd of the infamous "Merkle" game on October 8, 1908. In case you don't remember it, let us refresh your memory.

The Cubs and Giants found themselves deadlocked in first place at season's end and had to replay a game held two weeks earlier to a 1–1 tie—the "Merkle game." Over a quarter-of-a-million people congregated in and around the Polo Grounds in New York. Not everyone could get into the stadium, of course. The ones who weren't knocking down the centerfield fence or trying to burn it to get into the game retreated to any vantage point they could to see even a small portion of the contest; on subway cars, rooftops, pillars, etc. Several people were injured, and one man died, after falling from his "viewing station."

So we see that sports and fatal pandemonium have been bedfellows for a very long time. The Polo Grounds, where are they again?

Yes, Boston and Chicago and Detroit and Los Angeles fans, *et al.* have their moments of shame, but since New York fans are so fond of reciting history—albeit revisionist history—and incidents of violence that they, no doubt, are familiar with the occurrence of early Tuesday morning, October 19, after the Red Sox won Game Five of the 2004 ALCS in the fourteenth inning. Julio Rodriguez, Yankee fan, fifty-eight, murdered Sox fan Jose Rivera, thirty-three, and wounded two others on I-95 in Wilmington during an argument over the Red Sox game, according to a source involved in the investigation. (Boston.com)

As we said before, many teams have their bad seeds, but the fact is, *Sports Illustrated* (July 7, 2003) polled 550 major league players and the numbers came back to say that New York led the voting for city with the *worst* fans garnering 16 percent of the vote. It did not say whether they were referring to the Mets or the Yankees, but we're gonna go out on a limb here and guess the team from the American League. Hey, the players should know. Who are we to argue?

You're probably wondering if they're like this everywhere, when, if ever, is a good time to talk to them? During a game is probably a bad time, but there may be an exciting hardball contest playing out for your viewing pleasure. Don't let them deter you from partaking. And if you still want to go to Yankee Stadium, feel free. It's cheaper than a Paul McCartney concert and rarely sold out so you have a better shot at getting a seat. *(You also have a better seat for getting shot.)* And don't say we didn't warn you!

CHAPTER FIVE—
CLASS WARFARE

There is a common misconception out there that every conversation you have with a Yankee fan is the same: infuriating. But that is not always the case. Through rigorous studies here at *HTTTYF*, conversations with Yankee fans have been classified into four different categories. They vary in tone and aggression from the most docile Class I rating to a tumultuous Class IV, where you should immediately evacuate the borough before it explodes.

INDEX OF YANKEE FAN CONVERSATION CATEGORIES
Class I: The Look

A Class I conversation isn't technically a conversation at all. This is when the victim receives a knowing glance from a Yankee fan. Imagine you are wearing a Mariners jersey and you come across someone dressed in full Yankee regalia. Upon making eye contact, he or she will give you a look that says, "Poor Mariners fan. You wish you were a Yankee fan like me." Or perhaps this Yankeephile will actually *say* this leaving you speechless at such a brazenly cocky person.

Class II: The Repression

You can have a Class II conversation with a Yankee fan. It is not heated and at times, you believe the Yankee fan is making concessions. You can actually enjoy the discussion. Some people spend their entire relationship in a Class II with a Yankee fan. Married couples with kids are prime examples. The Yankee fan may even start the conversation by saying, "I'm a Yankee fan, but I'm a true fan. I rooted for them when they sucked" as if that has anything to do with how much you'll respect them.

Class III: The Dispute

(*6.4 on the Richter scale*) This is the most common of all *tête-à-têtes* with Yankee fans. It starts with a right and a wrong. They're right and you're immeasurably wrong. There is no gray area. The Yankee fan is never willing to cede his or her point, even with irrefutable proof dictating otherwise. You'll notice seven typical stages to this conversation, as a non-Yankee fan tries to interact with the Yankee fan.

Seven Stages of Talking to a Yankee Fan in a Full-on Class III conversation

1. Polite Correction—With the motive of being helpful, kindly informing the Yankee fan of his misstatement and supplying a more accurate version of it. "Well Craig, I've given what you said a lot of thought and, with all due respect, allow me to make one minor correction; Billy Martin is *not* the greatest manager *alive*. I hate to break it to you but he died in 1989."

2. Interpretation—A restatement highlighting the major points of interest to clarify any part that may be vague. Again, done with kid gloves. "Mike, when I said, 'the Yankees did, in fact, have a higher payroll than all other teams in nine out of the past ten years, I meant that they spent MORE than other teams, not less as you seem to think.

3. Recitation of Facts—The fan is convinced that you are speaking hypothetically or with an opinion. This is where you must provide evidence that you are speaking objectively with stats, numbers, names, etc. to back up your statement. "I'm sorry Jennifer, but I can prove to you that Derek Jeter does *not* have the best ass in the game. In fact, the latest *Sports Illustrated* opinion poll gave that honor to Albert Pujols."

4. Repetition—Perhaps he didn't hear you the first time. Pavlov found that in a controlled environment, doing and saying things over and over again will force a subject to conform to the repetitive actions the same way jack-hammering a block of cement will

cause its form to change. In other words, keep saying it and the conversation will progress. Whether in a positive direction or negative remains to be seen. "Listen Al, I'll say it until I'm blue in the face; you are dead wrong! There was no government conspiracy to 'let the Red Sox come back from an 0—3 deficit.' No, there was not! Look, I'll sit here all day if I have to . . . "

5. Automatic Contradiction—The two of you will volley back-and-forth expressing your opposing views. "Am not!" "Are too!" "I'm rubber, you're glue . . . " "I know you are but what am I?" "You're an ass—quitsies." "You didn't call it! *I* call quitsies." "You can't call quitsies." "Can too!" "Cannot!" Etc.

6. Incredulous Revelation—At this point, after exhausting any amount of reasoning you may have had in you, you will convey your disbelief that your efforts have been fruitless up until that point. "I can't believe you could possibly be this stupid! The Yankees have gotten WAY more calls in crucial situations than AGAINST them. How is it possible for one man to live with his head up his ass for so long?!"

7. Severance—The going of separate ways, locked in a bitter standstill. "I'm done talking to you. It's pointless." "Good! I have nothing to say to you anyway." "Fine." "Good." "So get out of here." "It's *my* house." "Fine, I'm gone. This place sucks anyway." "No, *you* suck anyway." "No, *you* suck . . . "

Abner Doubleday suggests . . . When talking to a Yankee fan, substitute big words with small one-syllable grunt-like noises.

Class IV: The Assault

Picture Falujah, now add *even more* hatred. This one only ends one way—badly. It's started by a Yankee fan whose only desire is to goad you into a battle either through intensely annoying chants or statements or by borderline offensive and immature actions. They never really wanted to talk anyway. It's called the "Iraq Resolution" because there will be a war, even if one of the parties is complying with the laws.

> **FUN FACT:**
> *Many people don't know that a Class IV conversation was essentially the impetus for the Cuban Missile Crisis between Sox superfan John Kennedy and Yankee aficionado Nikita Khrushchev. Khrushchev developed his love of the pin-stripers from baseball player-turned-dictator Fidel Castro.*

Being able to determine the type of conversation is important in dealing with Yankee fans. It's the difference between bothering to get involved and not. Learning the categories, you will realize that most random, nonsensical statements fall under Class III. Unless, of course, the Yankee fan is foaming at the mouth while speaking; then it's a Class IV. (Scientists here at the institute have been unable to develop a vaccine for this particular strain of Class IV, but with the help of government grants and continuous generosity from the public in the form of tax-free donations, we grow closer everyday to eradicating it once and for all.) Whichever the level, proceed with caution.

Talking to Yankee fans is not for the faint of heart or the novices. You can't just jump into conversations with them with your rudimentary knowledge of language and grammar. Yankee fans require a different approach. So, as children learn to write and speak early in their development, we shall afford you the same practical approach for preparing your encounters with Yankee fans—Mad Libs!

We've already supplied you with a list of adjectives in Chapter One that you can employ below. The rest of the exercise will give you an idea of the tone of a discussion with a Yankee fan. We suggest you photocopy the page so that you can practice several times until you feel you are ready.

YANKEE MAD LIBS

It was a typically __(adj.)__ day in the Bronx late one spring as the __(major league baseball team)__ came to town. Two guys, Steve and Alan, were in town for the annual __(occupation)__ convention and as luck would have it, their team was playing at Yankee Stadium so they decided to take in the game.

After paying a scalper __($$)__, they found their seats in the right field bleachers, right behind the __(noun)__. They weren't seated for thirty seconds when Alan pointed toward the aisle. "Hey, look at that guy __(-ing verb)__ on the __(noun)__", Alan said. "He's so __(adj.)__ that I bet he __(verb)__ right over here."

Steve turned to look and immediately had to cover his nose. "What is that __(adj.)__ stench? It smells like a(n) __(insect)__ crawled up a wino's __(body part)__ and __(past tense verb)__ while a(n) __(housepet)__ was __(-ing verb)__ on __(famous person)__."

The Yankee fan, who obviously had too much __(intoxicant)__, stopped next to Steve and Alan, swaying for a moment trying to regain his balance. "Ay! What the __(expletive)__ are you wearin'?! We don't want any of that __(expletive)__ piece of __(expletive) + (excrement)__ here."

"Hey, we're not looking for any __(noun)__" Alan reasoned. "We just want to watch the __(noun)__ and may the best __(noun)__ win."

He slurred, "Well, that'll be the __(expletive)__ Yankees, you __(adj.) + (expletive) + (feminine hygiene product)__ bag!"

And with that, the Yankee fan, who looked sort of like a cross between a(n) __(farm animal)__ and __(dead politician)__ with a belly that looked like he was smuggling __(plural noun)__, took a handful of greasy __(food)__ and stuffed it in his __(adj.)__ face. He

shouted, "Your _(expletive) + (city)_ sucks a big bag **of** _(expletive) +_
(endangered species) + (body part) ."

Alan, feeling a little more confrontational, puffed out his chest
and said, "What do you know? You're just a __(adj.) + (venereal dis-_
ease) infested Yankee fan. I bet you don't even know who's pitching
for your team."

The Yankee fan took to the offensive and screamed at the top of
his lungs, "Who gives a flying __(expletive)_? You can take your
__(expletive) + (noun)_ and shove it so far up your__(expletive) +_
(body part) that _(bodily fluid)_ comes out of your mother's _(exple-_
tive) + (body part) ."

Everyone turned to see where the noise pollution was emanating.
"Real nice," said Steve, "and right in front of __(famous Roman_
Catholic cardinal) . Real classy."

"You want class, go back to that piece of _(excrement) + (city)_
that you call home and do the world a favor and jump off the _(exple-_
tive) + (renown bridge) . And that goes for you too, __(expletive) +_
(famous Roman Catholic cardinal) ! Go back to Rome and tell the
Pope he can take his _(expletive) + (religious artifact)_ and ram it up
his_(body part)_!"

And as the __(adj.)_ Yankee fan took a step to confront Steve and
Alan, he __(past tense verb)_ and __(another past tense verb)_ until
he hit his head on a __(noun)_ . The nearby fans cheered as the
security guard escorted him out of the stadium.

[NOTE to publisher: this line below is not going away.]

Because the Yankees were losing at the time, their _(synonym for_
"bandwagon") fans naturally left early. And so, Alan and Steve
were able to move down behind their team's dugout and enjoyed
the remainder of their time at the ballpark. By the way, the _(team_
name) wound up pummeling the Yankees _(large number)_ to _(low_
number) and all was right in the world, if only for one day.

THE (expletive) END

CHAPTER SIX—
OUT OF THE MOUTHS OF BABE'S FANS

We have come to the meat of the tutorial: the entree, if you will; a part crucial to your apprenticeship, so do not tune out now. This is what we've come to expect from a Yankee fan: A fresh plate of drivel with a side order of nonsense. Let's break down the cause of the dissention and rub out the rhetoric. Then we can talk to them. We're just *talking*, okay, so put the bat down!

Yankee fans are, first and foremost, arrogant, and second, obnoxious. But "arrogant" and "obnoxious" are habitual bedfellows. Usually one is not "arrogant and sweet" or "arrogant and delightful." (Although, it can be argued that after the Yankees blew the only 3–0 lead in baseball history, Yankee fans were found to be "arrogant and reticent.")

Normally, it's in their nature to constantly let you know where you stand in relation to them. There is a method to their demeaning madness, however. They manage to fool themselves into believing that they are more knowledgeable or diplomatic than they actually are. It's like they're looking into a fun house mirror. Hence, you never know what is going to come out of their mouths, but you can be certain they didn't consult with their brains before they opened their jaws. So . . .

WHAT'S THE STUPIDEST THING A YANKEE FAN HAS EVER SAID TO YOU?

Hi, I'm a Yankee fan.

— *Brandan Ahern, Shrewsbury, MA*

A Yankee fan has never said anything intelligent to me; therefore I have no point of reference for this question.

> — *Adam Sivits, Brooklyn resident*

After the 2004 ALCS, some drunk fan said that I "must be a queer" because I like the Sox. I'm not gay, but I still couldn't figure out the logic behind that comment.

> — *Alex Emanuel, actor/musician, NYC*

Anything written by Filip Biondy of the *New York Daily News*.

> — *Gregory Faherty*

Because I said so.

> — *Yankee fan to Davy Marsh, when asked to justify his statement that the Yankees are the best*

Davy, living in New York City, you must already know that this witty rejoinder is usually followed by yelling, "Oh, yeah?!" louder than you.

Now you may be asking yourself, how do Yankee fans manage to keep their distance from reality?

In 1996, this institute created a department called the Idiosyncratic Department located in the Bill "Spaceman" Lee wing on the third floor. The department was charged with the task of observing and categorizing behaviors, speech-patterns, and idiosyncrasies unique to Yankee fans. Their findings have pin-pointed nine distinctive characteristics in their behavior. These behaviors lead to the following devices of trickery which they utilize copiously. Knowing these tricks is half the battle, as it will allow you to prepare yourself in advance. In some instances, you can cut them off before they can get started.

PLOY #1: SAYING THINGS WITH CONFIDENCE

Confidence is a good thing. Everyone should drive down the Confidence Beltway to Self-Assuranceville, but if you get off an exit too soon, you end up toiling around in Cockytown on Arrogant Lane. Yankee fans have a summer home there. And they're not about to sell it. Not wanting a debate, but rather, they only want their views heard.

D. Snow, Yankee fan AND New England Patriot fan (how is that possible?) expressed some rather eclectic views when ask about the infamous Don Zimmer/Pedro Martinez "scuffle."

> Zimmer was trying to make a point about throwing near a player's head because of what happened to him before. It should have been up to the umpires to prevent it from getting to the point that it did. Actually, Manny is the one to blame. He overreacted to a high fastball and was just looking for a fight.

Let's take a moment here. Zimmer isn't at fault for attacking Pedro, but MANNY is; Manny Ramirez, the Boston outfielder?! Too bad we don't have footage of Manny whispering in Zim's ear in that broken English coaxing the grizzled bench coach to charge at Petey like a bull in Pamplona.

Of course, the second part of that statement is so inane that you might actually skip over the first part—the part about Zimmer making a point because of what happened to him. True, Zimmer was once hit in the head himself, so we can imagine he is against the ritual of throwing up and in, but Clemens is as notorious as Pedro at that practice and you'd be hard pressed to find footage of Zimmer charging the Rocket when the latter played for New York.

When Clemens drilled Piazza, Zimmer said, "Piazza wasn't a man for complaining about it." Then, when one of his guys gets hit, Zimmer suddenly decides that pitcher is a "headhunter." What a joke!

— *Gianni Monteleone*

"You're JUST Jealous of Yankee Fans"

They're practically begging for a snappy riposte. Don't hold back. Enjoy your penalty shot, unguarded.

Why? Your city smells like pee.

— *Jon DeStefano*

Yeah, I wish I had the bad hair and Jersey accent.

— *Raj Nath*

That's like being jealous of a boil on your ass.

— *Ben Hill*

Have you seen 'em? It's like ugly gas was dropped on the Bronx.

— *Adam Sivits*

I also hate Charles Manson. Am I jealous of him too?

— *Laurie Russo*

PLOY #2: THEY ALWAYS ASSUME THE OUTCOME WILL END UP IN THEIR FAVOR

Boston fans were a nervous wreck attending Game Four of the 2004 ALCS at Fenway Park. The tension was palpable to begin with but then throw in loud-mouthed Yankee fans who had already decided the series was theirs.

As Jim Chilson tells it, "Five Yankee punks would stand up and yell, 'Hey, Bobby, which World Series game do you want to go to, Game Two or Game Six?'"

Hmmm, we wonder which game they went to. Where do they get the balls, you might ask? That attitude comes from the top. Take for instance, the letter that the Yankees issued to their suite holders regarding postseason ticket information. It went out before September 20, when the Yankees trailed the Boston Red Sox by a half-game in the American League East (Boston.com, September 27, 2005). The memo began: "The New York Yankees are entering the post season for the eleventh consecutive year." Don't imagine that Oakland, Boston, and Cleveland thought too fondly of that memo as they all had designs on being in the post season too. The numbers were going to allow only two teams in.

PLOY #3: SAYING THINGS WITHOUT THE FACTS

These may sound like silly ramblings to a lot of us, but to a Yankee fan, it is a powerful talking point. Are they misinformed or just plain uninformed? With a desperate need to acquire the facts, that's where you come in. Your job is to inform them. As much as they'd like to rub it in, it just isn't happening with their twisted logic which could be the main reason why they get so annoyed with others. Nobody likes to feel stupid. But we'll leave the dime-store hypothetical psychoanalysis of a Yankee fan to Dr. Phil and his book *Dime-store Hypothetical Psychoanalysis of a Yankee Fan*.

If someone does not bother to find out when he is wrong, then he isn't wrong. And that is the Yankee fan. It's reminiscent of Wile E. Coyote walking on air. Only after learning about the law of gravity, did he plummet to the ground and land with a resounding splat. And so, with this unsubstantiated blowhardedness, if you'd like to call it, you couldn't convince some Yankee fans of the simple laws of logic, even with a topographical map.

During the Red Sox victory parade after defeating the Cardinals in 2004, Pedro Martinez was hit with a baseball as he rode along in the procession on one of the city's famous "duck boats." Yankee fans quickly labeled that as reckless celebrating that endangered people's lives (something they know a thing or two about). Forget the fact that all accurate accounts tell us that a fan was simply tossing a ball to Derek Lowe to have it signed. Why let facts get in the way of a good rumor? They had the main points—the ball, Pedro's Geri curl, and a fan. Close enough.

PLOY #4: TAKE ANY OPPORTUNITY TO BERATE OTHER TEAMS, ESPECIALLY THE RED SOX

We're already familiar with this one from Phil's response in our first chapter regarding the correct way to refer to his ilk. Similarly, in September 2005, a radio talk show host in Concord, New Hampshire was asked the following question pertaining to the way the media describes thing:

> **Caller:** Why do they say stuff like this quote in today's *Boston Globe*? "Baltimore's Eric Byrnes snapped a 1-for-37 skid with a seventh inning double." The guy is now 2-for-38. I don't think he snapped anything. I await your response.
>
> **Host:** It fills a sentence. There is no validity to claim that a single in the midst of a 1-for-37 slump does anything more than give a momentary respite from his stretch of awful play. While playing better in print, no one has the guts to print the truth, least of all the morons in the *Globe* who are too busy trying to make David Ortiz out as the American League MVP.

Phew! That one kinda sneaks up on you, doesn't it? Can you tell that our New Hampshire sportscaster is a Yankee fan? Yankee fans constantly claim never to care about Red Sox fans yet, they have to get a dig in every chance they can. You could be at Sunday school—

> Okay class, can anyone tell me who convinced Eve to take the apple from the tree of life, thus securing lifelong banishment for Adam and her?
> The snake?
> No, actually, it was Curt Schilling.

They don't spend anytime thinking about other teams at all . . . Yeah, right.

PLOY #5: HYPOCRISY

This one is the most stunning. Don't be rendered speechless or expect a punchline after they say it, cuz you'll be waiting a long time. Crickets will even get tired of chirping before a Yankee fan admits, "Oh, I'm just screwing with you; I didn't really mean it."

"You guys are losers for getting so excited about one championship"

Keith Camire quickly countered, "At least that's one championship you'll never see!" Zuty correctly pointed out, "The only thing that makes one a loser is losing." And Paul Suchecki responded with an appropriate analogy, "Getting to home plate with one's girlfriend doesn't make it less sweet."

And I guess you guys didn't have a parade in 1996 when you won your first in eighteen years? We presume there's a protocol now for celebrating championships. It's become like finding the appropriate gift for anniversaries.

NUMBER OF CHAMPIONSHIP	TRADITIONAL CELEBRATION
First	Milk and cookies in city library
Fifth	Congregate in park, sing "Kumbaya"
Sixth	Down shot glass filled with Boone's
Tenth	High-five people on street
Twelfth	Tip over cars and burn things
Fifteenth	Detonate atomic bomb
Twenty-Sixth	Endlessly recite how many championships your team has won

My boss is a German Yankee fan (they say two negatives make a positive—not in this case) and I tried to explain the significance of '67 and '75, getting out of class for the Dent fiasco of '78, the christening of the Buckner Tunnel, and to see my grandfather trying to hold on 'til the Red Sox won the big one. All this meant nothing to her as she bitched back, "The Yankees have von more World Se-rays and you make such a bic deal about vinning von?"

— *Sparky Schneider*

She's absolutely right, Sparky. You were celebrating as if it were your team's twelfth championship whereas it was only their sixth. (SEE: celebration chart) *Mea culpa*!

Other topics Yankee fans like to bring up with no regard for the hypocritical aspect of things include: how other teams have sloppy players, Clemens' reputation as being a headhunter *until* he got to NY, the uncouth language at other ballparks, and, of course, their favorite—ANY argument regarding money and team salaries.

Certain events have occurred over the past few years that allow Yankee fans to renege on their previous stances in favor of a kinder, gentler, more pro-New York stance, i.e., the Yankees failure to win.

> A lot of my relatives root for the Yanks. My cousin Joe, in particular, loves to rag on my dad and me. Every gathering we have to endure the customary, "Yankees are superior because . . . [Insert diatribe here]." He'll also call and razz my dad whenever the Yanks are winning. However, when my team wins, he can't be reached for days."
>
> — *Kate DiStefano*

Really? You're saying a Yankee fan can dish it out, but he can't take it? Nooo . . . That's tragically shocking! [NOTE: Enough sarcasm to fill the Hudson River.] Ask a Yankee fan if they like to rub it in and their answer differs from Kate's experiences. "Oh, no, we'd never do that," they claim. "The hurt is already too deep. There's no need to rub it in," says Yankee fan Steve G. And if they lose, "I realize how tough it is for them to cope with not being a Yankee fan and how big a thing it is for them to beat us. So I congratulate them with a handshake and a look in their eye," says Jon N. (It comes off pretty good on paper, doesn't it? Try to hold them to it and it's a different story.)

Abner Doubleday suggests . . . Using non-alcoholic beer when drinking with Yankee fans.

So how do you avoid these little zig-zags? One, the most obvious way is to stop talking to them. But the other way is to call them on it. Chances are, they won't notice what they've done, or at least they won't acknowledge it, but now it's out there.

PLOY #6: IRONY

Similar to being hypocritical, their ironic statements hint at a biting wit, if only Yankee fans saying them were in on the joke. They have less of the two-faced, scornful attitude than their hypocritical cousins have.

> Isn't it funny how Yankee fans who always maintained that they don't really care about the rivalry and that the Red Sox are just another team to them, then turned around and said that losing to the Marlins [in 2003] didn't matter because it was all anti-climactic after beating the Red Sox? I heard this a lot, and yet none of them seem to be aware of the contradiction.
>
> — *Angelica Fisichella, Boston, MA*

Ah, irony. Is there no greater literary style fraught with humorous and rhetorical effect?

PLOY #7: FEIGNING SYMPATHY TO GAIN YOUR TRUST

Sometimes, they all can seem like *Tearjerker Jerks*, letting their guard down to attend to your emotional needs. Misery loves company and they're here to point out your misery.

"I've been a Yankee fan through the lean Years"

There are more examples of people who *think* there are actually some good Yankee fans out there. And there might very well be. However, one caveat—there are those who will claim to be "true" Yankee fans and *not* bandwagon jumpers, but they always take the wrong approach citing, "Hey, I've been a Yankee fan through the lean years!" It only serves to anger their protagonists . . .

> Right. 1986 was tough.
>
> — *Raj Nath, supply chain consultant*

> Really? And when was that?
>
> — *AJ Poulin*

By "lean years," do you mean "the Mattingly years?" How overrated is he??!!

— *Jon David Chesloff*

There are half a dozen teams whose entire existence have been "lean years."

— *Adam Sivits*

What lean years? You've always been fat.

— *Ben Hill, Mets fan*

The statement makes them seem even more arrogant and less sympathetic. They don't know what lean years are, compared to others. Our recommendation to Yankee fans: Just say, "I've been a fan since the '80s." That's enough for the baseball fan populace to respect you just a little bit more. But if you end that sentence with the year "1996," there is actually a law in New England that makes it legal for natives to rip out your tongue and feed it to the sharks at the New England Aquarium.

PLOY #8: TAKE COMMENTS ABOUT THEMSELVES AND ACT LIKE THEY PERTAIN TO OTHERS

You've heard of this technique before. It's very "Sean Hannity." They listen to the barbs and jibes about the Yankees and themselves. They memorize them and just substitute another team in the place where the word "Yankees" should be. Since the Yankees are ridiculed a LOT, there are a lot of phrases that they have to choose from. Some classics you may have heard before:

- "You guys are ruining the competitive balance of baseball."
- "Your fans are all a bunch of thugs."
- "Your fans are all a bunch of bandwagon fans."

(Believe it or not, that last one was uttered as recently as September 2005 to a gaggle of Red Sox fans. We find it hard to fathom how some people can wait eighty-six years for a World Series championship and then be labeled as "bandwagon fans," particularly by a Yankee fan from Rhode Island.)

Minnesota Twins fan and deep thinker, Doug, sees right through this tactic:

> When Yankee fans call the Red Sox "the *new* Yankees," [for winning with a high payroll] it is a really a clever ploy to keep the Sox and their fans as subordinates. Don't be fooled. They have their own identity. They are not the new anything. They simply are.

But the all-time gold star winner for this ploy:

"The umps were bought"

When asked if the umpires seem to make more bad calls against them or for them, Yankee fan Jon Neuhaus brazenly responded with a concise, "against."

No fans use this excuse more than fans of the New York Yankees. And they have *less* reason than any other team to say this. That complaint ain't gonna fly with Padre, Orioles fans and Red Sox fans and Mets fans, or any other. Derek Snow is reluctant to use that excuse as often as many Yankee fans, but he still turns a blind eye. "I think it evens out. I've seen some horrible calls go against the Yankees and some horrible calls go for them."

Steve Grinsted pleads the fifth on this, but he does use it as an opportunity to unleash Ploy #4, taking a shot at the Red Sox. "I've never noticed if the Yankees have more calls go against them or for them. But I have noticed that Red Sox fans tend to blame the umps for their lack of success . . . that's a shame."

Remember, they rarely spend time thinking about the Red Sox. Yet, thoughts about Boston manage to infiltrate their consciousness while answering other questions. Needless to say, all Yankee fans choose one of these three answers, none having the open-mindedness or desire to speak the truth. For examples refuting Yankee fans' claims about fairness, please refer to the "Blown Calls" sidebar at the end of the chapter.

It is the most annoying of all their ploys. And since they speak so confidently about things they know very little about, it can cause you to become more infuriated.

PLOY #9: BRAGGING ABOUT WHAT'S SUPPOSED TO HAPPEN

We may never understand their attitude toward winning. On the one hand, it's *their* team, the one that they've put all the emotion into, as have we for each of our teams. But on the other hand, it's not a question of *if* they're going to win as it is with all other teams. The mighty conglomerate puts the mom-and-pop store out of business . . . again. The varsity Division I-A basketball team beats the holiness out of the sisters of Saint Mary's. As Rick Reilly, in *Sports Illustrated* said, "If 'YANKEES WIN WORLD SERIES' deserves a headline, then so does 'BULLDOZER DEFEATS TULIP.'" (*SI*, 11/1/99)

They don't mind if their team is the bulldozer. A win is a win. But if they lose:

> They try to justify their losing, with lines like, "If you look at both lineups, it's clear the Yanks were the underdogs. It would have been an embarrassment if your team lost with *that* roster!"
>
> — *Ryan Walker, NJ*

That last one is a smorgasbord as it touches on #5, #6, and #8 as well—#5 because if you said it to them, they'd jump on you for being a sore loser; #6 because it's what everyone thinks about them; and #8 because they obviously heard someone using it before.

Now, with their tricks in mind, do you still want to talk to them? Of course, you do. You wouldn't be able to call them on any of it if you didn't. The fundamentals of talking to them are based on solid technique: **Breathe, think, converse**—all done at a relaxed pace with nothing to prove. Act like you don't care what they think. The second you start to get heated up it could get ugly.

There are three ways you can choose to proceed in any conversation. Say you find yourself embroiled in one of the discussion classifications from Chapter Five, you can . . .

Agree–Hey, great! If you agree, there's no work that needs to be done. Sit down and toast to critical harmony.

Counter–They say that Joe Torre is the greatest manager of all-time. You say, "That's not true, but here is a list of managers that could, in fact, be called the greatest manager of all-time . . . "

Dismiss–If his statement is so ludicrous that it'll waste too much time to bring him back to sanity, something like, "Don Mattingly deserves to be in the Hall of Fame" then just scoff, snicker, pivot, and walk away. You have more important things to do, like watching paint dry, counting the actual time they play music videos on MTV, or cleaning your privates with a cheese grater. Again . . . just walk away. Assuming the avenue you are most likely to navigate is "counter," you must be ready for a grind-it-out conversation.

> Any GOOD and TRUE fan *can't* let them win an argument. Whatever they throw against the wall, you come back with stats to back up your team such as the leaders in pitching, hitting, base hits, etc. . . . . Do whatever you have to do. Take no prisoners! They don't win the argument; they don't..
>
> — *Keith Camire, defender of good*

Well said, Keith. Do whatever you have to. Duck, dodge, parry, spin, turn, thrust! Don't relent. Remember, you have the forces of truth and justice on your side.

MORE HELPFUL HINTS FOR TALKING TO YANKEE FANS

To successfully converse with a Yankee fan, you must learn to fight fire with fire. Except that you need to make your fire intelligible and well reasoned, as Keith said, and be sure to give them everything but the last word. This will surely antagonize the average Yankee fan, as it should, cuz watching them detonate is good, clean fun. In fact, if the Yankee fan you're arguing with doesn't become thunderstruck with stuttering, impotent rage, you're not doing it right. Yankee fans, much like neoconservatives in the heated political climate, don't get angry when lies are told about them, they get angry when the truth is told about them.

We are exaggerating to some degree by condoning impotent rage as that's not conducive to a good conversation, but once you've laid out facts and corrected his mistakes, it's out of your hands. You can't control his reaction. Hope for the best, but expect the worst.

The conventional wisdom and philosophy for arguing with Yankee fans is simple: Tough love, without actually loving them. Put yourself in a Yankee fans' shoes. Ask yourself the following questions:

1. Does my opinion make sense?
2. Does it regard other viewpoints in a "fair and balanced" manner?
3. Could I possibly be wrong?

If you can answer "no" to all these questions, then you're thinking like a Yankee fan. If you answered, "yes" to each of those questions than you are not even close to thinking like one. You're thinking like a liberal. Knock it off!!! Have you not been listening to us at all?! I mean, Good Lord! What is the point of us trying to help you if you're not even going to listen?

So, to revisit the question, how do you deal with this on a mature level? What are some ways to silence them? Sure, you could emulate how Yankee-hating icon Jim Chilson handled those cocky punks and their bragging during Game Four of the 2004 ALCS:

> By the fifth inning, I'd had enough. Usually I'm very mild mannered and can take a lot of crap but this was the last straw. After they went on about "WE rule, WE this, WE that . . . " I stood up and said, "Listen, you little fucks, this WE shit has got to stop. You've most likely done nothing with your little lives. Especially you, mister 5'5", 165 pounds, you think you could be out there doing this? NO . . . ! So sit down and shut the fuck up, you little shit! You are nothing but a little pussy and you always will be!" Since I had a "24" road jersey on with Evans across the back, the crowd erupts and starts chanting, "Dewey! Dewey!"

— but that's not the direction you want to head in. We suggest a more traditional, verbal, and sometimes non-verbal, way of ceasing their speaking. (By the way, for all the praise those punks were giving themselves, do you think they took any of the blame for choking in the end?)

WAYS TO SILENCE A YANKEE FAN

Getting a New York Yankee fan to shut up is one of the great challenges in the world right along with climbing Mt. Everest with an elephant tied to your back, especially if they smell blood. If a Yankee fan senses that he or she has the upper hand, it is hard for them to relent. Their team is winning, their team has won, their team isn't even playing, but your team lost—all are sparks that cause a Yankee fan's mouth to ignite. Here are some tips to prevent them from thinking they got the best of you:

Avid Red Sox fan Bill Burr takes a zen-like approach with them. He gets a lot of practice spending time in NY. During the 2005 pennant race, Bill continued to be subjected to Yankee fans giving him crap. He makes a plea for you to follow his example which is endorsed by us at the *How to Talk to a Yankee Fan Institute*.

> They're so beside themselves that they can't make a Red Sox fan mad anymore, that if you just continue it by remaining calm and say, "What are you gonna do, chant '2004'? It's only been one year, who gives a damn? Nothing will change that even fifty years from now. And even if you win the World Series this year or next, no one will choke any bigger than you guys did in 2004; nobody in hockey, nobody anywhere in any sport. You're the biggest chokers ever." That gets them mad again. So I want you to promise that you're not gonna lose your temper around Yankee fans.

One final method, but not one that needs to be overlooked is employing a healthy dose of reverse-psychology. You might just want to let them have their happy little fairy-tale world with sky of green and Dandelions growing in the mahogany ocean. Try this:

> Tell them they are the best (which is SO hard to do) but it shuts them up for the time being.
>
> — *Davy Marsh, Braves fan and New York inhabitant*

Just walk away snickering before they have a chance to realize what you said. If you're still there, they will follow it up with, "Yeah, that's right! Say it again, bitch!" You'll be tormented for agreeing with him. Usually they are going to torment you one way or the other so you might as well confuse them until their head spins around and smoke comes out of their circuitry like R2-D2 in *Star Wars*.

Some people keep themselves blissfully unaware of a Yankee fan's mutterings. Paul Nardizzi, father of four, averred, "I don't recall ever listening to a Yankee fan. Sorry."

So there you have it, that's what you can expect coming from the mouths of Babe's fans. We've shown you a multitude of ways to sidestep their barrage of nonsensical refuse and verbally defend yourself. And as a last resort, you can prevent them from thinking they got the best of you by simply repeating everything they say like the reverb from Lou Gehrig's immortal speech. If that fails . . . ah, what the heck, go ahead and pick up the bat!

BLOWN CALLS

In big games, the calls pull more weight and they are more memorable, as they take place on the national stage. We remember Kent Hrbek lifting the runner's leg off of first base to tag him and on an even grander scale, the 1972 U.S. Olympic basketball team falling to the Russians after actually *beating* them. The eyes of three or four officials can momentarily stray from where they need to be and these things can happen. But when you talk about the Yankees and the breaks they've gotten over the years, you have to wonder. We're talking about a *string* of big games where calls have suspiciously been called in favor of the Yankees. Yes, there have been calls against the Yankees that seemed unjust, but can you recall any in the playoffs?

Along the run of New York's most recent string of pennants, one can point to instances of outlandish calls that led to a swing of momentum towards the pinstriped palookas. And in any sport, momentum is key.

1998–Game One, a strike on Tino Martinez is called a ball allowing him to get a payoff pitch. It seems everyone in the universe knew it was a strike, except strangely, the home plate umpire.

> I was nineteen in 1998, the same age as the number of my favorite player, Tony Gwynn. And with that one pitch, I knew he was destined to be ring-less his whole career. So when I moved to New York in 2002, my hatred for the Yankees had been planted for a long, long time. Every time I saw that damn N and Y having incestuous sex, my eyes turned red, Red Sox red.
>
> — *Adam Sivits, Padres/Red Sox fan*

1999–An ALCS saturated with glaring umpiring errors (what would that be on your scorecard, E 10?), the final straw forcing normally restrained Boston fans to toss debris onto the field during Game Four.

> It started in Game One. Top of the tenth, the Yankees Chuck Knoblauch allowed Scott Brosius' throw from third on John Valentin's grounder to pop out of the webbing of his glove, but second-base umpire Rick Reed blew the call, deciding Knoblauch was transferring the ball to his throwing hand and calling Offerman out on a force.—(*USA Today*, Oct. 1999)
>
> Game Four, eighth inning, New York clinging to a 3–2 lead, second-base umpire Tim Tschida called Boston's Jose Offerman out after Yanks second baseman Chuck Knoblauch tried to tag Offerman and missed as Offerman was trying to advance to second base on John Valentin's one-

out grounder. The sweeping tag was a good two feet from hitting anyone. From every angle of every replay, including the POV of the moronic umpire making the call, Knoblauch whiffed and only got the force out at first. This would have brought up All-World shortstop Nomar Garciaparra with a runner in scoring position and two outs. Instead this botched call resulted in an inning-ending double play. And then an inning later, when Nomah did bat, he was called out on a close play at first base. The game was stopped and manager Jimy Williams was ejected for arguing the call. Fans at Fenway Park then threw bottles and other objects on the field, causing the Yankees to go back to the dugout for several minutes.—(*USA Today*, Oct. 1999)

You can say it was the curse at work, but the only curse that week was a strangely homogeneous incompetence on the part of the men in blue favoring the Yankees.

And the granddaddy that started them all:

October 9, 1996–Baltimore versus New York. Twelve-year-old, Jeffrey Maier, reaches out and takes a harmless fly ball to the warning track away from Oriole right fielder Tony Tarasco. Umpire Rich Garcia awards the Yankees a tie game and having their lead taken away penalizes the Orioles by taking away their lead. It was a real momentum killer for the O's, one from which they would not recover.

All ballparks have a rule where if you interfere with a ball in the field of play, it results in your automatic ejection from the stadium. It's on the back of your ticket. Evidently, not in Yankee Stadium. Or so it seemed. (Keep reading.)

Although these are the events that stick out in most people's minds, since they came at crucial moments, there are times when the baseball justices in the sky try to level the playing field.

> *August 30, 1997*–Not even a year after the Maier debacle, interleague play brings the Expos to the Bronx. Pedro Martinez (at the time, an orphan) is on the mound mowing down Yankees. Darrin Fletcher gave the Expos all the offense they needed with a three-run homer to right field on a play where the ball was snatched from Paul O'Neil's glove by a fan.

In case you were wondering, the fan that took the homerun away from O'Neil was escorted out of the building. Hmmm, that's strange, you say? But we thought Yankee Stadium allowed fans to stay on the premises after catching home run balls. Ask Yankee security and they'll reply that Maier was not led out because no interference was called and therefore there were no grounds to eject the youngster. (*NY Times*, 8/20/97)

Well, interference was *not* called during the Expos game either. Talk about a double standard! (No, really . . . talk about it.) We guess the hypocrisy (Ploy # 5) comes straight from the top and trickles down to the fans. An ejection only applies if you do something to *hurt* the Yankees. For the illegal act that Maier did, though most likely with no knowledge he was interfering, not only was he *not* punished, but he was made a hero in New York City, proof that they'll praise lawbreakers if they help the Yankees win. Look at Maier's appearance on the *Today* show if you question that or the fact that the firehouse in his hometown displayed a huge banner praising his actions. Sad.

> *September 7, 1998*–Bernie Williams drifts back to the triangle in Fenway Park, glove up, poised to make the catch on a deep John Valentin fly ball. A fan wearing a yellow-colored top reached out with both hands, his arms extending over the wall and downward, and hauled in the baseball. (Though reports weren't sure if it was, in fact, a Boston fan or a New York fan who was the culprit.) (*NY Times*, 9/8/98)

Those last two are the calls Yankee fans refer to when they talk about the umps being bought. Of course, a call in August or September versus a call in the playoffs is a toughie. We kinda think getting the call in October carries a little more weight.

Conspiracy theorists used to say that the umpires were too afraid to make a close call against the Yanks in Yankee Stadium. And we've seen what their fans can do so we would understand if that were true. But lately, the calls, *correct* calls, have been going for the opposition, robbing fans of what they believe is their right to always get the calls.

In recent times, fans of the Bombers have been left speechless when umpires confer on the mound and then, without the benefit of the dozens of replay angles we have on television, rule in favor of the visitors. And the replays show a play consistent with the ruling. Take Todd Walker's homerun ball that snuck inside the right field foul pole in the upper deck during the 2003 ALCS. The play allowed us to see how blind Yankee fans are to the truth. While replays were showing the television audience that it was a fair ball, a spectator in the area where the ball landed was asked his thoughts and he was *positive* it was a foul ball. Nice try, sport.

And lest we forget about A-Rod running up the first-base line toward the ball in Red Sox pitcher Bronson Arroyo's glove.

Yankee fans were speechless when umpires brazenly reversed the "safe" call in favor of the correct one. Unfortunately, their arms weren't rendered useless as well and they managed to litter the field with debris in disgust. They just don't like the rules, unless the rules favor their team.

This evidence proves the point that Yankee fans are negligent in acknowledging the truth about whether or not umpires make more bad calls for them or against them.

CHAPTER SEVEN—
I HEARD IT THROUGH THE GRAPEVINE

E-mail is another avenue that Yankee fans try to take out aggression as they type away on their keyboards while secluded in their mother's attic. The idea is that they will type outrageous, offensive things and leave thinking that they are brilliant. Any responses that come back to them in the form of a correction are simply dismissed or used as grounds for more outrageous statements.

E-mail provides an anonymous forum for you to be anyone you want and say anything you want. It's the cyber equivalent of "ding dong ditch." Most of the stuff you see is not even worth responding to. Look at the bad grammar, the lack of an intelligent thought, the bad language . . . Either the screenname belongs to a Friggin' Ute or a convict typing from the prison library.

If you've got time to kill and want to get a kick, sure, write back and see what the response is. But don't expect to get a Mensa–echelon dialogue going.

E-mails either end with the offending party signing off in a "ding dong ditch" fashion or sticking around for banter with a willing participant in the back-and-forth. In that case, it usually doesn't go too long before one or both parties end up bored. NEVER does the offending party admit, "Damn, you got me with your logic and forethought. I was wrong to say those things earlier. I apologize." Only in a dream world, perhaps a world where every major league team has a chance to win each year and steroid users face a greater punishment than those who bet on baseball games in which they weren't involved.

Typical qualities demonstrated in an e-mail by Yankee fans include, but are not limited to: denial, rationalization, hypocrisy, unfounded braggadocio, short temper, backhanded compliments, sympathy, and complete insanity.

There is no way to try to educate the users of message boards. If they wanted to be educated, they would proceed out into the world for such lessons as: "The English Language—Vowels are your Friend," "How to Wean Yourself off Breastfeeding," and a necessary course for any serial poster, "Leaving your Bedroom for the Real World."

The following series of messages will give you the best methods for responding in the chess-like world of message board posting. Again, you cannot expect to win anything here, only to amuse yourself and, with a little bit of serendipity and some creative phrasing, infuriate the Yankee fan.

These were plucked directly from web posts during the 2004 Red Sox/Yanks ALCS through the World Series versus the Cardinals as Yankee fans continued to harass Sox fans. They appear exactly as they were written: with all the venom, hypocrisy, bathroom language, and typos that make this rivalry truly captivating and decisive, if not juvenile.

GAME 1, OCT. 12, 2004 SOX LOST 10–7

Choke Sox Going Down!!!—Posted by nanzero - Oct 13, 12:07 am
nice game lossers. it going to be at least another 87 years

Posted by oker - Oct 13, 12:09 am
Don't you mean just '87 years'?

Posted by nanzero - Oct 13, 12:12 am
that's what I said moron

Posted by oker - Oct 13, 12:15 am
No, "another 87 years" would mean 173 years total.

Posted by redsoxusa - Oct 13, 12:19 am

That's just an example of Yankee math.

Posted by nanzero - Oct 13, 12:22 am

yeah like 26 for the yanks + 0 for the sox

Posted by oker - Oct 13, 12:27 am

Hey nanz, you still crunching the numbers on that? Need an abacus?

THE CORRECTION

It could be an incorrect fact, bad grammar, or in this case, their math. Ignore what they're trying to say and focus on their execution. It's similar to the non-sequitur technique used frequently in *Monty Python and the Holy Grail*.

GAME 2, OCT. 13, 2004 SOX LOST 3–1

Who's your Daddy now? Posted by braytonlee - Oct 14, 1:25 am

Poor Pedro. Yankees ALCS . . . 2 down 2 to go . . . looks like this is the end of the road for the Red Sux!

Posted by Krissie - Oct 14, 1:31 am

you want to be a follower . . . cheer for the Yankees, you want to be a true fan and stick by your team no matter what . . . cheer for the Red Sox!!!!!!!!!!!

EXPLOITING WEAKNESSES

Yankee fans are renowned for jumping off the bandwagon at the slightest incident proving their fallibility. Make that the focus of your reply. As her team was down two games to none at this point, Krissie set out to take away braytonlee's upper hand.

Posted by brambillo - Oct 14, 1:34 am

actually, if u want to be a lozer and spend your entire pathetic life hoping for something to happen that has no chance in hell of happening, cheer for the sox. if your from new york and want to be true to your roots, cheer for the yanks. "COWBOY UP YOURS" u stupid fag sox fans

Posted by Globby - Oct 14, 1:36 am

"COWBOY UP YOURS" HAHAHAHAHA lol—funniest thing I've ever read!!!!!!

Posted by conigliaro - Oct 14, 1:38 am

That's only 'cuz you just learned to read earlier today!

THE KICKER

Let it play out and wait for your opening. Use Mohammed Ali's rope-a-dope strategy if you have to. This poster obviously was following along and chose the perfect moment to make his presence known. One punch, one knockout.

You'll notice there were many opportunities to make corrections from the possessive "your" in place of the contraction "you're" to the word "lozer." These *faux pas* are ripe for parody. But what would it get you? It's clear that brambillo leads the pathetic life so why join him.

GAME 3, OCT. 16, 2004 SOX LOST 19–8

HA HA HA!! Posted by sockssuck - Oct 16, 11:58 pm

The only thing that would've made this game better is if you got 10 more runs so the score would've been 19-18. Get it?

Posted by hodiguy - Oct 17, 12:02 am

No, could you explain?

Posted by sockssuck - Oct 17, 12:05 am

'cuz you pinheads haven't won in over 75 years and it wont be another 75 'til you win again! 1918, 1918 . . .

Posted by hodiguy - Oct 17, 12:07 am

Thanks, I never could've put that together on my own. And you're right; it won't be another 75 years. Maybe it'll be this year.

Posted by sockssuck - Oct 17, 12:10 am

Yeah right. Go have some more clam chowdah.

Posted by KevinR - Oct 17, 12:14 am

There is so much pride in Yankee fans until they start to lose, then they jump off their own bandwagon. And brilliant slam with the "clam chowder" line! I don't think he can recover . . .

Posted by hodiguy - Oct 17, 12:17 am

You're right; he nailed me. I'm gonna log off now. If only I could remember where I left that damn soup ladle.

SARCASM

It is a sign of intelligence and feel free to whip it out any time the conversation allows. Take your time with it. Walk them through the solution. The only problem here is . . . Yankee fans might not be able to pick up on the sarcasm and think that you're being serious. Hence, the post is intended for only those observers who can read between the lines.

GAME 4, OCT. 17, 2004 SOX WON 6-4

Yankee Pride - Posted by starkraving - Oct 18, 1:24 am

You sox losers can say whatever you like . . . you only won 1 game. no team has won more Championships than the Bronx Bombers. Enough said.

Posted by luvbugg - Oct 18, 1:26 am

Typical Yankee fan. They lose just one game and immediately have to talk smack and remind everyone about how great they once were. Let us focus on the present and remember that Rivera is Boston's bitch!

THE POINT-BLANK CALL

Note the form and technique of this Yankee fan. Whatever happens in the present, he brings up the past—the modus operandi of any Yankee fan. That's when you call them on it. Describe to them how the world views them. Read on and you see how it angered a few more of them.

Posted by yanksrock - Oct 18, 1:27 pm

Hey dipshit why don't you just root for your red sox and not against the Yankees? Your obviously letting out all the anger from the constant losing streak you've had for 86 years

Posted by gennesse - Oct 18, 1:28 pm

Same story, different year. It will be a sad day in Boston if the sox ever do win . . . All you "so called fans" will have nothing to talk about anymore.

Posted by randall - Oct 18, 1:29 am

2 words dude, YANKEES SUCK! its as simple as that

Posted by starkraving - Oct 18, 1:31 am

Yeah the Yanks suck and we make it to the post season every year. Grow up you fucking 12 year old. You won one fucking game. Yeehaw! There's no way in hell your gonna win another won. We shut you out tomrrow night on our way to #27! Suck on that!

Posted by dave52 - Oct 18, 1:33 am

Sox & Yanks fans represent the best and worst of baseball. Yes your rivalry transcends the sport and raises fan passions everywhere. However, both teams spend craploads of money that most other teams simply can't afford to do. By the way, swearing doesn't make you funny or cool on these posts, only immature.

Posted by starkraving - Oct 30, 1:35 am

2 words dude, FUCK YOU! its as simple as that

WALL BALL

Imagine a Yankee fan as a six-year-old child. (We know, not hard to do.) They stick their fingers in their ears and scream, "La la la, I can't hear you! La la la." They make you feel like you're simply tossing a ball against a brick wall. Nothing gets through. It just keeps coming back to you. Dave52 tried to bring the conversation back to the adult section, but he got rebuffed. Starkraving didn't want to go. Just keep hitting the brick wall with your ball.

Posted by shamalama - Oct 30, 1:37 pm

Wow, the class of Yankees 'fans' never ceases to amaze me.

GAME 5, OCT. 18, 2004 SOX WON 5–4

SOX FANS FUCKIN' SUCK!!! Posted by sockssuck - Oct 19, 11:40 am

big friggin' deal, you won 2 games. youre still gonna choke and fuckin' sox fans suck!!!!!!!!!!!!!!!!!!!!!!!!!

Posted by redsoxusa - Oct 19, 11:42 pm

Are you going to back that up with anything or let your ignorance speak for itself?

Posted by sockssuck - Oct 19, 11:48 pm

well you fucking do!!!!!!!!!!!!!!!!!!!!!

Posted by redsoxusa - Oct 19, 11:50 pm

Oh, I see. When you put it that way, who could argue? Simply dazzling.

Posted by sockssuck - Oct 19, 11:55 pm

What does you mean asshole!!!

Posted by redsoxusa - Oct 19, 11:57 pm

What I "does" mean, my intellectually challenged friend, is that you supported your claim with exactly what exists between your ears and legs . . . NOTHING! Try looking "sarcasm" up in the dictionary.

Posted by sockssuck—Oct 20, 12:04 am

Youre a douche bag.

Posted by redsoxusa—Oct 20, 12:06 am

Wow! And it only took you seven minutes to come up with that gem. You should be a filibuster.

Posted by sockssuck—Oct 20, 12:09 am

Fuck you.

Posted by redsoxusa—Oct 20, 12:10 am

Three minutes . . . you're on a roll.

BAIT-AND-SWITCH

Just like deep sea fishing, you dangle a little worm on the string and watch the Yankee fan latch on. This particular exchange is quite exemplary. One might even say the poster is a master baiter. Redsoxusa stayed calm while sockssuck was obvious too emotional to keep up until he was reduced to little more than a dejected curse. The switch part comes as the Yankee fan goes from aggressor to reactor.

GAME 6, OCT. 19, 2004 SOX WON 4–2

Posted by beerisgood - Oct 20, 2:12 am

HEY BRO CAN YOU SAY 3 IN A ROW? NEVER SO YOU CAN SHOVE THAT UP YOUR ASS. 26>1

Posted by tenuka - Oct 20, 2:15 am

We just won three games in a row, assclown.

Posted by beerisgood - Oct 20, 2:12 am

3 WORLD SERIES IN A ROW. CAN YOU SAY THAT JISM HEAD? 26>1

Posted by cabawaba - Oct 20, 2:15 am

I can actually: 3 in a row: as in the last three years that teams with significantly less payroll have kicked the shit out of the Yankees to win the WS. The Sox are about to make it 4 in a row. Can you say that?

Posted by beerisgood - Oct 20, 2:18 am

YEAH, LIKE THAT'LL HAPPEN IN A FUCKIN MILLION YEARS. KEEP DREAMING. 26>1

Posted by cabawaba - Oct 20, 2:21 am

All those years and you still can't figure out how to work the "Caps Lock" key.

Posted by Kolami - Oct 20, 2:23 am

He's too busy using all of his brain-power to get his index fingers to fingers to find the "2, 6, & >" keys, which he will most likely wear out.

Posted by soffit - Oct 20, 2:23 am

This guy is like Forrest Gump when he started running everywhere for no apparent reason. My guess is that he'll eventually move on to something else. Let's just be patient, he might even be paroled by then. Post Forrest . . . Post!

Posted by beerisgood - Oct 20, 2:29 am

26>1 WORLD SERIES! GOODBYE LITTLE BOYS 26, 26 , 26, 26 . . . .

Posted by soffit - Oct 20, 2:31 am

I guessed wrong.

THE GANG-UP ON THEM

Make it like a chat room if you can find other like-minded individuals around you. Enjoy yourselves as you take turns ripping your enemy. There was also an opportunity here to correct beerisgood when he claimed the discrepancy between championships was twenty-six to one. At that time, it was actually twenty-six to five.

GAME 7, OCT. 21, 2004 SOX WON 10–3

Yankee Fans - Posted by saintjames - Oct 22, 12:45 am

Awwwww too bad. Who's your daddy now? Or should I say who's your caddy? 'Cuz the Yankees will be on the golf course and the RED SOX will be still playing ball. WOW first team in HISTORY to loose a 3-0 lead. Yet another reason why the YANKEES SUCK!!!

Posted by dusty - Oct 22, 12:47 am

How's George doing after his "all-time choke team" failed to beat Boston by dropping the last 4 games?

Posted by nybrother - Oct 22, 12:49 am

He's laughing his ass off that his team fell to the world's greatest FLUKE job in the history of sports! ONE HIT WONDERS!!!!!!!!!!!! THAT'S HOW YOU'LL BE REMEMBERED!

Not many people know that Denial River flows right into the Hudson and slams against the banks of the Bronx. Poor nybrother didn't know how to react so he lashed out.

Posted by jasonf - Oct 22, 12:52 am

4 wins in a row is not a fluke. It's a fact that equals a championship, which the Spankees have none this century.

Posted by starryeyed - Oct 22, 1:05 am

It was good baseball and the better team won. anybody can lose 4 in a row

Posted by ticketmaster - Oct 22, 1:08 am

Yep, that's why it has never happened before. When you have the worlds best closer on the mound and he blows it, it's a choke job no doubt. You are right about one thing; the best team did win.

Posted by rapman - Oct 22, 1:10 am

hey ticket head, Rivera is still the greatest closer in MLB history! and yeah, he's fucking human. he just lost two family members before the series and he's supposed to just wipe that shit out of his head?? you tard!

Posted by striderite - Oct 22, 1:12 am

Wait just a second dill-hole, what about Game 1 when he didn't even get to the park until the 3rd inning, then still got the save? Man you have a terrible memory.

An excellent example of a hypocritical statement by a Yankee fan. Striderite was right to call him on it. Rivera didn't seem to have any trouble in Games One and Two. But it suddenly became a burden in Game Four?

Posted by rapman - Oct 22, 1:15 am

i realize he got the first save jackass . . . but the shit weights heavy. It finally caught up to him by Game 4. But a red neck shithead like yourself wouldn't know shit like that! WHAT DO YOU HAVE . . . LIKE A 4TH GRADE EDJA-MACACION???

Posted by dkny - Oct 22, 1:16 am

If anyone is acting like a stupid redneck it's you, pal. But hey, have fun watching us in the WS this week

Posted by nybrother - Oct 22, 1:19 am

Yeah we will. And for your team it is a FLUKE and you're going to prove it to the entire world this week when you get swept in the WS! Then, everyone all over will know it's a FLUKE! Face it; you're never going to get that lucky again!

There's some unfounded braggadocio, otherwise known as trash talking. He was sort of right though; he did predict the sweep.

From what we've seen so far, you can clearly see the pattern that both Sox and Yankee fans fall into. Both camps claim to possess a commanding knowledge about all things baseball. However, in these posts, very little time is spent on the specifics of the games. Both derail that train faster than a "wicked hammered" green line conductor. The instant after the final out is logged into the record books, they begin verbally (and sometimes physically) abusing each other before the tarp is dragged out onto the field and used to cover the skeletons of umpires who dared make calls against the Yankees.

The next series of posts are from the days following the World Series. Sure, Sox fans may be gloating a little, as well as they should. In addition to the triumph of "good over evil" and the monumental win, it was also a small victory for the rest of baseball to watch Red Sox Nation expose the Yankee's Achilles Heel.

OCT. 27, 2004 SOX WIN WORLD SERIES 4–0

Sox still suck!!! Posted by hampshirehound - Oct 27, 11:40 pm

big deal so you beat the cards who suck anyways. The yankees would have won too and they <u>didn't</u> choke. You guys got lucky with bullshit calls and dumb luck. The yanks are the greatest team ever, not the chokers the choke-sox are every year after year . . .

This is a classic example of rationalization; a step beyond denial in that he's accepted that it happened, but determined it was due only to outside forces. Hence, it wasn't earned. It's also nice to see they have internet access at Bellevue.

Posted by redsoxusa - Oct 27, 11:42 pm

Okay, let's assume you're right and the Yankees are the greatest team in sports history and they didn't choke. Well, we just beat them. By your reasoning, that would make us better. No?

Posted by hampshirehound - Oct 27, 11:45 pm

No. 1 little world series win and you same idots that were hiding 10 days ago are now on top of the world with knowledge . . . the yankees hold most records . . . .its obvious you are all jealous of them . . . .jealousy is a disease that few of you have caught it . . . baseball season is over . . . period

Posted by blahblahblah - Oct 27, 11:47 pm

Another great answer from a typical Yankee fan. Unless you are over 40 you have not seen shit from what the great Yankees have done. 2 rings in the 70's, 4 in the 90's, good but all you guys always do is play down everything every other team does. You've had the best team money can by for 4 years and won nothing. And I am not a Sox fan! I like the Twins.

Posted by KewlGurl - Oct 27, 11:50 pm

OKAY IF UR NOT A SOX FAN OR YANKEES FAN THEN GET THE FUCK OUTTA HERE! THIS IS FOR THE RIVALS BETWEEN YANKS AND SUX. NO ONE CARES ABOUT U TWINS!

Actually, we love the Twins; especially the mud wrestling ones in that beer commercial. By the way, this is textbook projection from any basic psychology course. KewlGurl took her anger at the Red Sox and projected it at this innocent Twins fan.

Posted by omar7 - Oct 28, 11:53 pm

Just out of curiosity, of these wondrous 26 championships, which ones weren't the most expensive teams during the seasons they won? They had the top payroll every one of those years! Like I've always said, Yankee fans just don't get it. Ruining baseball.

Posted by shiraz - Oct 27, 11:56 pm

What a dumb ass Moron. we haven't bought a world series in a long time, at least 4 years! Furthemore, the years our payrolls was overwhelmingly highest, we haven't won squat. Just enjoy your win, last won you'll see for another 86 years

This last post is unquestionably the best example of "Yankee Logic" we have yet seen. Let's break it down.

- A capital 'M' for 'Moron' but no capital 'W' for 'We.' *Okay, innocent enough.*

- "We haven't bought the Word Series for a long time, at least 4 years." *A full admission that they simply just buy their victories.*
- "Furthermore, . . . " *0-for-3 on grammar.*
- "the years our payrolls was overwhelmingly highest, we haven't won squat." *This is wrong on so many levels . . . but at the same time, just soooo right!*
- "last won you'll see for another 86 years" *Hasn't yet grasped the English language. But if his forecast for our future is anything like the other Yankee soothsayers in these posts, we may just look to repeat the next few years. Thank you for your wisdom, young shiraz . . .*

THE NEXT DAY . . .

Red Sox '04- greatest team ever! Posted by parader - Oct 28, 12:28 pm

Yankee fans can have your 26 titles, they are now offset by being the biggest disgrace in sports franchise history; courtesy of red sox nation. On the other hand, the '04 World Champion Sox are now and forever known as the greatest team, the greatest season and the greatest sports story ever told. Your curse has now begun, the curse of A-Rod, (or I should say "Purse of A-Rod", a silly little punk-ass-bitch slapping the ball from Arroyo's hands.) and the rest of the highest paid losers of all time. The Yanks are doomed for failure!

Posted by warrenbradley - Oct 28, 12:30 pm

I'm quite amazed at how quickly some Sox fans have become so self-confident. You should be celebrating your first championship in 86 years, not trying to one-up the Yankees. Taking cheap shots at the Yankees only shows that you still are inferior to us. Come on now . . . just shut up & enjoy your championship. And lets look at reality here; your 1st title since 1918 doesn't "offset" the 26 championships they won. They're still the most storied franchise in sports history. But I have to give the Sox credit for coming back from the 0-3 deficit. But they'd have to win many more WS champs to rank up there with the 1996-

2000 Yankee dynasty. And I wouldn't go overboard and call this season the greatest of all time either . . . the 1998 Yankees take that title. It was definitely one of the most compelling stories, but that's as far as it goes. Enjoy your title and start thinking about your own future instead of trying the disgrace the Yankees.

Even though he's out of his gourd with comments like "the '98 Yankees are the best team ever", we finally see a touch of logic and a modicum of intelligence from a Yankee fan. Maybe we were wrong about them as a group.

Posted by tommyngina - Oct 28, 12:34 pm

u boston fans are the alltime worst fans yeah the yankees choked but get real yankees will be back you willn't. go for vote for fagot kerry!

Oops, maybe not.

Posted by yukon - Oct 28, 12:37 pm

FYI, those little red and green squiggly lines under your text indicate spelling and grammar errors. They don't accentuate your point. Come to think of it, you didn't have a point.

Posted by tommyngina - Oct 28, 12:42 pm

niether did you fuckhead.

Posted by yukon - Oct 28, 12:43 pm

You just made my point.

Posted by konman - Oct 28, 12:45 pm

Dude, you're just wasting your time talking to yankee fans. No one likes them anyways.

Posted by boodiddly - Oct 28, 12:49 pm

Yeah, sit back and smile! Enjoy the feeling of being world champs & don't even let the thought creep in, OOPS!, there's it is . . . so this is a what Yankee fans feel like . . . WRONG!! we Yankee fans never sit around waiting for our team to blow it and we never have to pinch ourselves to make sure we're not dreaming . . . instead we always expect our Yanks to win and when they don't we go right back to default mode. now if one world series in the modern era eliminates all the doomsday thoughts that torment the minds of Sox fans, you might have a inkling of how we Yankee fans feel all the time. But I doubt it. See ya next season.

Posted by tooter - Oct 28, 12:54 pm

Guys I applaud the fact that the Sox won, as an avid Yankee fan since we sucked in the early 70's and into the 80's our owner has only done what your owners have now learned to do. Now the rivalry will be fiercer. It proves nothing to take childish shots at each other's players. These guys are motivated by money not the jersey they wear, believe me you would have taken A-Rod and Jeter too if you could. Just as we'd take Shilling, Pedro and Lowe. Great accomplishment, it hurts to lose to your rival, as you have felt, but it flatters us to know how deeply you feel about it when we win, it only proves the fear when you call us names or make crude remarks.

Posted by birdman—Oct 28, 12:59 pm

And I applaud a Yankee fan that articulates himself well. It's rare. You must be over 40.

Posted by tooter - Oct 28, 1:03 pm

That I am. And thank you for pointing that out that not all Yankee fans are bad.

DAY TWO . . .

Posted by deewayne - Oct 29, 1:43 pm

After reading these posts and seeing Sox fans say crap like "you yankee fans are just babies or why cant you guys just tip your hat to the sox?" Fuck the Red sox. Do you guys ever tip your hat to the Yanks? They've slapped your team around like a bunch of bitches for the better part of a century, and all you people ever say is they spend to much money. I won't give your team credit for what they achieve because they are my enemy. What kind of fan would I be if I didn't talk shit and support the pinstripes no matter what? The truth is we are rivals and no true yankee fan should be happy for your team. Wait 'til next year the Yanks will be back, and pissed. See you later bitches, and may this rivalry last forever.

Since Boston is done with the phrase "next year," you're welcome to it.

Posted by conigliaro - Oct 29, 1:44 pm

It has to be killing you to know that for at least the next 362 days the Sox will be the World Champions. And who knows how long you will own the title of biggest CHOKE ARTISTS!!!

Posted by firestein - Oct 29, 1:47 pm

While Sox fans deserve to revel in their great victory, it is pretty obvious Yankee fans are bitter. And I'm not a Sox fan. Sure they won 26 titles, but they were won by the likes of Ruth, Gehrig, DiMaggio, Mantle, and Reggie. They were a mini-dynasty through 1996-2000 with respectable players that even Sox fans can tip their hat to. But whose biggest off-season acquisition tried to "steal" the series away by slapping someone like a little bitch? Whose starting pitchers were so bad that the Padres starters are more appealing for a playoff run than Lieber, Brown, and yes, even Moose Mussina? Whose owner is the most hated man in sports? If you need to go buy Randy Johnson, Beltran or Delgado to make yourselves feel better, then you do what you have to do to. The Sox ended the curse and the Yanks and their $252 million man came 2nd to the "idiots". I respect some of the Yankee greats like Yogi, Whitey and Don Larson. But A-Rod, Posada, Cairo, Sheffield, and even your boy-toy, Jeter . . . I can only think about them blowing a 3-0 series lead for the greatest choke job in the history of sports. Congrats Red Sox and all you die-hard Boston fans. I'll tip my hat to you.

THE VOICE OF REASON

Rarely seen, but always welcomed on the message boards. There are so few people who want to spend time stating their views so eloquently mainly because their audience would not appreciate it.

Posted by Olsmokey - Oct 29, 12:25 pm

Windbag! try waiting another 86 yrs for the next w.s. ring? no more 1918 but how's "2090" going to sound at the stadium? priceless

Posted by nyrjismlickers - Oct 29, 12:58 pm

How retarded are u? he just said he wasn't a sox fan and you lay into him like a typical arrogant piece of shit yankee fan. what r u going to do now? no more 1918, no more "who's your daddy", no more curse. And what do you say? "Now u have 25 more to go?" Well you're FUCKING STUPID! This is our 6th WS and if u stupid fat idiot new yorkers knew how to do math it would be 21. u r all pathetic. You can't even show one bit of respect for the sox winning the damn title. U GUYS R CHOKE ARTISTS! The so-called "Yankee Machine" couldn't put away the "lowly" Red Sox and u had 4 chances to do it. and u think its luck we won? I am so sick of u yankee fans. Now with we winning it all I can say is increasing payroll won't do shit for your "team". So go get beltran, get pedro, you're still not a team through and through. go ahead and argue with me yankee fans because everything u say and do is wrong.

He started off very reasonably. His main purpose here was to correct Olsmokey, but he got a little carried away. Uh, breathe, Mr. Jismlickers, breathe.

DAY THREE . . .

Yankee Fans & why they don't understand Posted by omar7 - Oct 30, 5:29 pm

Yankee fans say, "Big deal we win all the time". Problem is they don't win the WS, they buy it. That's why the Sox fans love this so much. Yes, 86 years and the greatest comeback ever have added to the hype. But, the best part for Sox fans is that, once again, the team that tries to buy the WS every year has lost again and we help keep them from buying another title and sullying further the name of baseball. If NY fans can wrap their mind around the fact that Boston and the majority of America feel this way I'd like to see how they feel about all their championships. Hell, the curse even comes from the Yankees throwing around their wallet back in the day for Ruth, they couldn't win they had to buy a championship all the way back then. So tough shit on you Yankees fans because you'll never understand.

Posted by theBabe - Oct 30, 5:33 pm

Yeah, we win all the time, we buy championships. Same old Red Sox losers whining & yapping about the Yanks. Yankee-hater hats and Yankees Suck T-shirts. Pure jealousy. I can understand that coming from a Sox fan. Inferior in every sense of the word. Go to Yankee Stadium and search for "Sox Suck" T-shirts or "Red Sox Hater" hats. You won't find any. We Yankee fans don't care about the Red Sox! Not even for a second! We only care about winning. Whether it's the Angels, A's, Mets, or the stinking choke-Sox, we just want to win. You Sox fans root against the Yanks so much that you hardly have any energy left to root for your own team. I bet the majority of you losers would have been happy just to beat the Yankees and NOT the Series. Jesus what a miserable group. Duhhh! Hope you continue your obsession with the best team in history; The New York Yankees. Hope you continue your loser Red Sox traditions of whining about the Yanks. You're cursed with that burden for the rest of your pathetic lives. It'll be passed down to your kids too (Only if you have the sack to reproduce, which you probably don't) So go ahead Yankee-haters, you can lick my ass right now. Right there! Haaa!

Posted by cyyoung - Oct 30, 5:37 pm

For a guy (or whatever you may be) that was one lengthy message from someone who doesn't think about the Sox "even for a second." Just a sign of bitterness. You must be deaf and blind also A..hole. If you ever crawled out of the sewer called New York City & polled other teams fans you'd find they all share one common thread; EVERYONE HATES THE YANKEES!

Posted by jpgotrocks - Oct 30, 5:42 pm

And people all over the WORLD hate the U.S. too. When your #1 everyone is envious. You must be a Communist. It would be nice if reality had a salary cap and companies could only spend $X on salaries. That would be "fair" to you right? That's not reality. These teams that cant compete with Boston, NY, LA, Atlanta, there's 2 words for them; MINOR LEAGUES! There's a reason they call it MAJOR LEAGUE BASEBALL. Life is not fair, why should baseball be! Capitalism boy - if you got more fans and SELL MORE TICKETS and MAKE MORE MONEY - why should your fans have to settle for an inferior product. Unless you think it would be good to have 32 versions of the Brewers and Pirates out there!

Well, actually, given the very nature of the playoff system, the White Sox are #1. Then it was the Red Sox and the Marlins, and the year before that, the Angels, and the year before that, the D-backs . . . and no one seems to hate those teams!

Posted by giblet - Oct 30, 5:48 pm

Once again, more ignorant, self-absorbed Yankee fans puking up Stock Line #4 à "Our players are home grown therefore, true Yankees. You guys buy all of yours, etc." Did it ever occur to you mullet-heads, that ticket sales & revenues from your own YES Network not only cover your team's payroll they also pick up the tab for your farm team and your friggin' scouts. And also, those payrolls (NOT counted towards the Yanks payroll) are higher than most other MLB team's ENTIRE payroll. So, as you so eloquently put it, Duh . . . no shit you have the best farm team & the best homegrown players. I'm amazed any of you Cro-Magnons have the brainpower blink. Run along, you should be getting back to your cell now . . .

Posted by brownbag - Oct 30, 5:51 pm

You're crazy . . . The Sox bought it just like the Yanks do. Sure it wasn't QUITE as much Yanks, but Quit trying to play the underdog; no one's buying it, and no one's buying your team.

Posted by giblet - Oct 30, 5:53 pm

I didn't know it was for sale.

Posted by brownbag - Oct 30, 6:04 pm

alls I have to say is who's your daddy?

Posted by shamalama - Oct 30, 6:07 pm

Reality used to be a friend of yours, I am guessing here. The Sox are your daddies. See if you can follow: You lost; we won. You choked (at home!). It's a pretty safe bet to say you didn't think before you posted that. Nice job sparky. Oh, and you should get a refund on that book you recently purchased on e-bay, Al Sharpton's "How to speak and spell MO-Bettuh". It clearly isn't working for you. Do the world a favor and throw yourself off of the Brooklyn bridge. —- Pussy!

Posted by marvin - Oct 30, 6:10 pm

I'm not a Yankee or Red Sox fan. I am a die-hard Cubs fan and I got to tell to it's not so much that Boston actually won the World Series which in itself is an amazement, but the fact that the biggest collapse in the history of baseball happened and the fact that it happened to the Yankees with 190 million dollar payroll. Boston won this year they played as a team, and showed a lot of class. Boston deserves every bit of this WORLD SERIES CHAMPIONSHIP. There is hope for the CUBS !!!!

Posted by showmoney - Oct 30, 6:15 pm

Right or wrong, the COUNTRY now views the Sox no different than the hated Yanks. For years I've been telling everyone that teams like the Sox, Cubs & Atlanta are as much a problem in the economics of the game as the Yankees. Yet, it has remained fashionable outside of NYC to bash the Yanks and proclaim teams like the Cubs and Sox as lovable losers. Not true. They too are teams full of expensive mercenaries just like the Yanks, but they have lacked the ability to win. Until now . . . So forgive the rest of the baseball world if we don't share in your pleasure. You get what you pay for & the Sox are as guilty as anyone.

Posted by striderite - Oct 30, 6:16 pm

I'll tell you the difference and I should't have to remind you holier-than-thou, entitled fuckheads who live in a toilet known as NYC that your team is now considered the worst chokers in professional sports history. So Yankee fans resort to childish, annoying things like 26>6 because that is now the one and ONLY thing they have over the Sox. For what seems like an eternity Yankee fans have gone on and on ad nauseum with the 'curse' and '1918'. We've had to deal with it. Guess what. The shoe's on the other foot now, buddy.

Posted by kirk - Oct 30, 6:19 pm

you could not of said it any better. for the first time yankee fans are on the outside looking in and they don't like it much. get used to it! Its great that every time a team in any professional sport goes down 3-0 in a playoff series the media will remind us on radio, TV and in the newspapers that the only squad in any sport but hockey to achieve the impossible is the '04 Red Sox. And the '04 Yankees will live in just as much infamy. Year Two-Thousand!! (clap, clap, clap clap clap)

Posted by rapman - Oct 30, 6:23 pm

hey chuckie baby . . . .get used to losing like you red suckers are used to it??? one WS does not wipe away a history of sucking and choking! trust me . . . .losing to you losers in the ALCS doesn't constitute a losing season! it was still a great year . . . that's what were used to . . . great years and if a WS comes along . . . that's just icing on the cake! now chuckie . . . .go back to giving your father his sponge bath!
"Losing to you losers." Brilliant!!!!

Posted by yanksrock - Oct 30, 6:13 pm

its the boston fans without class the second they win the world series they go straight to talking shit about the Yankees You never see us when we win the world series chanting "Yankees Suck". shows a ton of class for you Red Sox fans

Hmmm, so Yankee fans don't chant "Yankees suck" after they win the World Series. What's wrong with these people?

JUST PLAIN SILLY . . .

DAVID ORTIZ ARRESTED!!!!!!!!!!!!! Posted by curse1918 Nov 7, 9:07 pm

Sources say David Ortiz was arrested for breaking into a fudge shop in the Dominican Republic yesterday. He allegedly went home to visit relatives, but decided he'd rather sit his fat ass down and eat for a few days instead. When Cops entered the shop they reportedly saw Ortiz with no pants on eating fudge. He fled, but quickly ran out of breath and collapsed. Authorities cite the medical condition as "way too f*cking fat". However, no charges were pressed for undisclosed reasons. Ortiz later commented, "It's fun sucking dick, but even more fun when you have a mouth full of fudge." Red Sox GM Theo Epstein later said they are proud of Ortiz's comments because they feel he represents the values of everyone on the team.

Posted by striderite - Nov 7, 9:10 pm

#1 - He's in Japan you moron. #2 - Isn't it about time you changed your name? 1918 is old news buddy.

Posted by curse1918 - Nov 7, 9:12 pm

typical red sox fans, thinking that they know what they're talking about. 1) No shit he's in Japan. There is this nifty thing called a plane though. But your right, I doubt they would let any 600 pounders on a plane, the seats probably cant support the weight. 2) They won this year, but that's the only time since 1918. The Sox have now been upgraded to the 2nd worst team ever (over the Cubs). Congratulations! It's so obvious that you guys suck even by the way you celebrate . . . What rookie bitches. And after a great hard fought series, the classless spick Manny had the cute Jeter playing gold sign. He impressed me more that he can actually read, write, and spell, than what he said on that sign you f*cking tool. Long live the Empire.

Yes, "typical Sox fans" actually being intelligent and figuring out the Ortiz story was made up. It's the insane that look around and see the rest of the world as crazy. Racism and insanity usually ride together on the same bobsled.

Posted by trekker - Nov 7, 9:16 pm

A minor correction. The worst are as follows: 1. Cubs 1908 2. White Sox 1917

Posted by steviejam- Nov 7, 9:16 pm

If I could find you right now I would punch you in the face about 50 times. No need to be a racist and call Manny a spick. We don't need that shit on this board. You have some serious problems dude.

Posted by jimdandy - Nov 7, 9:20 pm

Dude, don't let that shitbum get on your nerves. Just ignore him. His team is the biggest failure in the history of opposable thumbs.

Posted by trekker- Nov 7, 9:24 pm

Are you saying that the loss by the Yankees, a team, playing a GAME, is greater than ANY failure throughout the history of mankind? I think that you need to get your priorities straight.

Posted by jimdandy - Nov 7, 9:27 pm

Ok, you win: The Yankees have been upgraded to the worst choke artist of all time. Congrats!

This one disintegrated real fast. Note how trekker tried to play the voice of reason. He succeeded in reaching jimdandy.

Now if that verbal gymnastics bout laced with sarcasm and pep-
pered with poppycock didn't kill off your remaining brain cells, go
have a beer. You deserve it. On second thought, that may be the
cause of this whole mess in the first place . . .

CHAPTER EIGHT—
YANKEES SUCK!!!

Dead of winter . . . not a baseball in sight . . . riding the Green Line to work . . . Everyone immersed in their papers, books and headphones . . . or staring off into space waiting for the Dunkin' Donuts coffee to take effect. Then out of nowhere, I hear a voice from the back of the train, "Yankees Suck! Yankees Suck! Yankees Suck!" And within seconds, I'll be damned if every last person on that train did not join in!—*Aaron Lyons, Woburn, MA*

Since the Babe's departure on that fateful day of January 3, 1920, these two words have rolled off New Englander's tongues quicker than their own native "clam chowdah." But it did not become the official hymn of Red Sox Nation and baseball fans everywhere until Labor Day weekend, 1998. *(See story)* The over-emotionally inspired "Yankees Suck!" chant has now become one of the fieriest and most debated matters between these two rival fan bases. And there is no gray area. Most Yankee fans will spend hours and hours telling you how stupid the chant is and how they never even give it second thought. Hours and hours . . . not a second thought . . . hmmm . . . I think we struck a chord.

Bronx native, Randy Ferrara, unwittingly provided us with a wonderful example of Yankee fan hypocrisy, "It's the dumbest thing I've ever heard in my life. It's so pathetic when they yell that bullshit, even when they're not playing us. We won twenty-six World Series and that's the best they can come up with? We don't suck! Ya know what? The Red Sox suck . . . dick!"

Our immediate reply, "Can we use that?"

"You can shove it up your ass is what you can do with it!"

Whereas Sox fans, on the other hand, seem to be split down the middle. Much like the comedy stylings of Carrot Top, they either find it juvenile and utterly repugnant or, they happily warble every letter as if it would guarantee them a seat at the right hand of the Lord (which there's no proof that it doesn't). We asked fans to share their thoughts on this storied topic. Here's what they had to say . . .

DO YOU PARTAKE IN THE"YANKEES SUCK!" CHANT?
I DO PARTAKE

I definitely participate in the chant. I feel that some of the Yankee fans aren't aware that they suck and it is my God-given duty to enlighten them.

— *B.J. Cook*

Definitely! And it's not about being literal. Obviously, they don't "suck" in the literal context. They suck because of their arrogance as a franchise, they suck because they always get the breaks (see *Blown Calls*) and, they suck because they don't care that their gigantic payroll is bad for baseball.

— *Matt Kennedy*

The best "Yankees Suck!" chants take place at Mets-Yankees games, where there is an amazing cacophony with half the stadium screaming "Let's Go Yankees!" followed by the other half responding "Yankees Suck!" I'd assume that we were working together if I didn't know any better—that's how good it sounds.

— *AV, Mets fan*

Yes, whenever one breaks out because they do. They just fuckin' do.

— *Adam Sivits*

When the mood is right; I don't like giving them the satisfaction of knowing we're thinking about them when they're not around.

— *Greg Prince*

I love it. It warms the cockles and subcockles of my heart.

— *Bill Abelson, singer*

I do. It was funny when the Patriots won their first of several Super Bowls and the victory parade is highlighted with the "Yankees Suck" chant.

— *Dustin Millman*

It is my automatic response whenever anyone starts talking about how great the Yankees are.

— *Gregory, Mets fan*

Only when I'm at the game, or watching the game in a bar, or whenever I'm awake.

— *Pete Deisroth, ski coach, Salt Lake City*

I do partake. It's a fun way to get out your hatred for the Yankees.

— *Davy Marsh, 15, NYC*

Absolutely. I think it should be the Massachusetts state motto—it would look great on a license plate!

— *Jimmy Dunn,* author of *Funny Ball and* former host of *NESN's Fan Attics*

I think everyone knows it's not the Yankee team that sucks. We chant it because they *don't* suck. But the way they were so good sucks. And that's what sucks about them . . . their essence.

— *Jon DeStefano, Boxboro*

Yes, sometimes it just feels good when I get stressed or angry. Like the other day I had to return a phone at Best Buy and they wouldn't take it back because I didn't have the receipt. I argued back and forth with the lady but she refused to give in. Finally I just looked her in the eye and said, "Yankees suck!" grabbed my broken phone and left the store. It was well worth it!

— *Juston McKinney, Saco, Maine*

I Don't Partake

No, I do not partake. I'd like to say it's because I'm a journalist, therefore trained not to betray my bias. Really, though, I'm just a pussy.

— *James Sullivan, journalist*

Absolutely not! It makes the greatest fans in the world look like idiots. Come on, Boston is a smart town; we can be more creative than that!

— *DJ Pare, Boston*

No, I'm not fond of negative cheering. The Yankees do obviously NOT suck. I might acquiesce to a "Devil Rays suck!" chant, but only because it's usually true.

— *Brian Cimmet, New York, NY*

Never. It is undignified.

— *Paul M. J. Suchecki*

No, that and the wave are two of the worst things ever created.

— *Paul Nardizzi*

I don't partake in the Yankees suck chant because that would be like picking on a retarded person. The Yankees don't suck. They're corrupt, greedy, and they have a monumental park celebrating their past. Meanwhile, they've been using a DH since 1973, something Babe Ruth, Mantle, DiMaggio, and most of the people in their early "dynasty days" didn't have the luxury of, so how can they really value one group of titles alongside the next when there's a giant schism in the way the game was played in the different eras?

— *Gianni Monteleone, Mets fan*

I take "suck" to mean lack of skill. Chanting "Yankees Suck" would make me feel like I was stooping to a Yankee fan's level of discourse. Come on; rise above it!

— *Ben Hill*

No, I do not take part in the chant. I savor the victories and accept the defeats as all part of the game. Of course, I don't like the Yankees and hope they fail miserably every year, but chanting and petty name-calling won't further the cause.

— *Sean Lambert, 27*

That chant is the worst chant in professional sports history. The Yankees don't suck. They've won twenty-six titles. If they suck, where do we stand? The only time that chant was appropriate was after 2004's collapse. In those last four games, they truly sucked.

— *Bill Burr, comedian*

YANKEES SUCK!–BY THE BOOK
Suck (sk) v. **sucked, sucking, sucks**
1a: To draw liquid into mouth by movements of tongue and lips that creates suction. 2a: Draw in by establishing a partial vacuum: *cleaning device that sucks up dirt.* b: Draw or pull as if by suction: *n.* The act or sound of sucking. **Phrasal Verb:** To take advantage of, cheat, swindle. **Vulgar Slang:** To be disgustingly disagreeable or offensive. To perform fellatio on. (*If you think the latter definition was a joke, please consult a dictionary near you.*)

It can be argued that, by the "phrasal verb definition" (the first part) and their numerous bush-league antics on the field that the Yankees most definitely do, in fact, suck. However, we realize their illustrious post-season record would indicate otherwise.

But it is the vulgar slang definition (again, the first part) that provides the proof to the claim that they suck. As evidenced by our fan responses, it's quite apparent that "the chant" is aimed *not* at the team, but directly at the Yankee *fans* themselves. (But to chant "Yankee FANS suck" would not have as much of a ring to it.) And by all definitions, *they* most certainly do suck. We've known it all along. We've said it in passing, we've said it out of frustration, and we've said it to make ourselves feel better . . . at least for the moment.

For you historians out there, here's a little tale you might not be familiar with, it wasn't until the fall of '98 that those magical words became the official mantra of Red Sox Nation and were publicly unleashed for the first time by lifetime Sox fan and Bostonian, "Gator" O'Previdi. This is his story . . .

VINNIE "GATOR" O'PREVIDI: INVENTOR OF THE "YANKEES SUCK!" CHANT

Vinnie "Gator" O'Previdi *nee* Vincent Patrick O'Previdi, was born on a makeshift cafeteria table at the Institute for Advanced Dental Studies in Swampscott, Massachusetts on September 11, 1969. He weighed 12 lbs, 3 ozs.

His father, Fitzy O'Previdi, a die-hard Sox fan and spot welder of Irish-Italian descent (*"Old McWop," as he'd refer to himself*), once bowled a perfect game while playing for his league's winning team, "Somerville Lumber." His mother, Maria, is a seamstress from Fall River by-way-of-Portugal. Fitzy and Maria met backstage at a Bad Finger concert in early '67 and were married in late '71.

Vinnie was the second of three children; all were breech births. His parents noticed he developed a severe case of "middle-child syndrome" as early as two-and-a-half years before his younger sister, Maria, was even born.

A garrulous and rambunctious child who often suffered from mild neuralgia, he was twice expelled from kindergarten: once for melting crayons on the radiator and, another time for repeatedly giving several of his fellow classmates both frontal *and* atomic wedgies. His love for anatomical repositioning was deemed so cold-hearted, so reptilian that his peers dubbed him, "Gator," a moniker he still uses today.

On June 10, 1975, Fitzy piled the family in the fire-engine red Datsun B-210 and made the pilgrimage to Fenway, where a young and excited Gator experienced his very first Red Sox game: a twi-night double-header against the Milwaukee Brewers. He recounts that "coming-of-age" virginal baptism thusly:

I remembah my dad gettin' us to the pahk wicked early to see battin' practice and shit. There was hahdly anyone else in the yahd. It was wicked pissah! Anyways, Bernie Cahbo hits a foul ball dingah towards us so I go sprintin' afta' the thing. My first day evah in Fenway and I'm like two steps away from catchin' a ball! Then I slip on a fuckin' Sports *Bah* wrappah, bang my head off a fuckin' rail and chip a fuckin' tooth. I don't remembah much afta' that.

Far worse tragedies were yet to befall upon the boy. In late August 1987, after at least a half dozen beers, seventeen-year-old Vinnie, seated directly behind Pesky's Pole at a meaningless Sox/Tiger's game, quickly rose to his feet when a Chet Lemon blast rocketed towards Boston's second most famous pole (Yaz being the first, of course). Hoping to avenge his childhood demons, "Gator" sought redemption as he desperately leapt to snag the foul ball. But the elusive orb was wind-blown just shy of clearing the fence and, having leapt too far, Vinnie took a nasty tumble over the wall and wound up writhing in the fetal position on the field.

As he lay there in a drunken heap, his friends lent their enduring support by rhythmically encouraging, "Gator, Gator, Gator . . . " When outfielder, Mike Greenwell, rushed over to help Vinnie to his feet, more fans had joined in, "Gator, Gator, Gator . . . " Those precious words echoed throughout "the Chapel" and made their way up into the broadcast booth where color-man Ken "Hawk" Harrelson mistakenly announced to all those tuned into WSBK TV 38, that the Fenway Faithful were paying homage to Greenwell by chanting "Gator, Gator, Gator . . . "

From that day forward, "Gator" was Greenie's nickname to Red Sox Nation.

Immediately following the game, an irate Vinnie, feeling betrayed by his friends (*in his own words*), "Beat the livin' piss outta those friggin' fuckin' cawksuckahs!" He has not spoken to any of them since and will go to his grave contending, "That cawksukah Greenwell stole my fuckin' nickname. I'm the fuckin' Gay-tah and I'm not fuckin' droppin' it!"

September 6, 1998, a day that would live in infamy. It was the day that the perpetual and appropriate "Yankees suck" anthem came to be. It was a day not unlike most other New England days, it rained for a while, and then it snowed a bit. Suddenly, the temperature soared to a record setting 103 degrees with a barometrically low dew point. Then it hailed. Next, the sun broke through for a moment, followed by a heat-lighting storm, more snow, hail again, and finally, scattered clouds with a light mist that would prevail for the rest of the evening.

Game on!

As dusk approached out on Boylston Street, Vinnie entered WAAF's popular "Fenway Frank Eating Contest." The first prize winner would receive four front row seats to that evening's Sox/Blue Jays game.

Even though the Sox were a remote twenty-three games out of first, rendering the game pointless, second place was not in the "Gator's" vocabulary. He ate like a carnivorous hyena in a feeding frenzy, inhaling an unprecedented sixty-three hot dogs (with bun) in forty-nine minutes and fifty-two seconds, shattering the thirty-seven-year-old tri-county record.

An hour later at the game, on a full moon night, from his Grand Prize-winning seats in the bleachers, directly behind the bullpen screen, Vinnie ordered beers eight and nine along with his sixty-fourth Fenway Frank. He recounts the conversation with his friend Mark much like this:

Vinnie: Hey Mahk, while you're up, get me two more fuckin' bee-ahs and a fuckin' dawg. And slap some fuckin' mustahd on 'it.

Mark: C'mon Gay-tah, you just ate sixty-three fuckin' dawgs, for fuck's sake!

Vinnie: What ah you, my fuckin' mutha', you retahd? My fuckin' dawg eating skills just got us in the fuckin' ball-yahd . . . for fuckin' free!

Mark: Awl right, you mutha' fuckah . . .

Mark begrudgingly obliged. All was right in Vinnie's world, at least for a few more innings. But by the seventh, Vinnie could sense trouble brewin' in the stands.

The Sox trailed 7–1 and the crowd of some 32,374 strong was out of kilter. A dilapidated beach ball sailed into the bullpen, abruptly halting the crowd's infectious game of volleyball. The wave became mired in the ennui of the right field grandstands, a Fenway first. And more importantly, Pete Schourek just caught Carlos Degado looking with the bases loaded to get out of a jam that nobody seemed to notice. For all eyes were fixated on the scoreboard—the icy harbinger of ill tidings. It showed the Yankees had just clinched the AL East pennant for the thirty-second time. The crowd was so hushed you could hear a church mouse let one rip on Yawkee Way. And smell it too.

None of this sat well with the Gator. Maybe it was indigestion from consuming dogs sixty-five thru sixty-eight the previous inning. Maybe, though he was shut off in the middle of the fifth, it was the booze talking. Or maybe, according to his court-appointed attorney and, corroborated by his psychiatrist at Brigham and Women's Hospital, his childhood demons were coming back to haunt him.

Whatever the case may be, at that very moment, Vincent Patrick "Gator" O'Previdi had an epiphany.

With a beer in each hand, he stood, perched high atop his chair, and roared to the crowd with the same unbridled antipathy that Maximus bestowed upon Commodus at the Roman Coliseum:

> What the fuck is wrong with you fuckin' people? You're actin' like your fuckin' dawg was just run ovah, you buncha' fuckin' loozahs! We were fuckin' mathematically e-fuckin'-liminated in April. So what, who gives a fuck? It ain't ovah "til that fuckin" fat chick in the green dress two sections ovah stahts singin'! Why the fuck can't you cawksuckahs just enjoy one fuckin' game heah . . . at fuckin' Fenway . . . in the fuckin' bleachahs . . . have a few fuckin' Fenway Franks and a few dozen fuckin' beeahs? Fuck the fuckin' Yankees! They fuckin' suck anyways! Do you fuckin' cawksuckahs hear me? I said: THE FUCKIN' YANKEES SUCK!

The best response Vinnie could earn was a slight murmur from the restless crowd. Unrelenting, he persisted. "Ah you fuckin' retahds listenin' to me? I said, 'Yankees suck! . . . Yankees suck! . . . Yankees suck . . . '"

And then an amazing thing happened— a few diehards, too tired to fight the unmatched passion of this inebriated cretin, almost involuntarily mouthed the words. Even fewer dared make them audible. And now a pair of fans together picked up the cadence, then a group, then a gaggle, until the entire section bought into it. And slowly, miraculously, from the bleachers, to the 600 Club, and to the rats behind the scoreboard, those words began taking flight . . .

"Yankees Suck! Yankees Suck!"

And it grew . . . and grew . . . and grew some more.

"YANKEES SUCK!!! YANKEES SUCK!!!"

The Gator's deeply profound words had blossomed into a thunderous cacophony that swirled like a funnel cloud hovering over a midwestern trailer park on a muggy July afternoon. Unfortunately, he had passed out by that point. However, every other man, woman, child, invalid, and third base coach in Fenway Park let rip from their lungs . . .
"YANKEES SUCK!
YANKEES SUCK!"

The chant stumbled into the Cask n' Flagon, had a few belts, and made its way outside to the peanut vendors, policemen and European tourists. Then it hopped the green line to Cleveland Circle where a pod of BC sorority girls were gussying-up for another night of keg stands at Delta Upsilon and a total loss of self-respect—all inexplicably started chanting those "forever-to-be-immortalized" words: "YANKEES SUCK! YANKEES SUCK!"

And just like that, a mantra was born.

*A passed-out Vinnie was escorted out of the stadium. His friends retrieved him from the Fenway security office following the game. Sox lost 8–7. To date, he still has no memory of this event yet maintains that Mike Greenwell stole his nickname.

CHAPTER NINE–
YANKEE SPIN ZONE

The best thing about working here at the *How to Talk to a Yankee Fan Institute* is the field work. In the evenings and on weekends, our staff of 535 punches out, yet continues to think about their job.

> My mother always said, "Find a job you'd do in your spare time."
>
> — *Jeff Ludlow, informational analyst*

Even while socializing, our "scouts" find themselves engaged in conversations with Yankee fans. That's where much of our knowledge comes from—first-hand accounts.

Back at the office, the experience comes out into journal after journal entered into our Microsoft Access database system.

> I've found myself getting into some pretty heated debates with Yankee fans, but I didn't care if I won or lost. All I could think about was getting to my computer and jotting the whole conversation down.
>
> — *Molly Kemp, editor,* Yankee Fan Quarterly

In this chapter, we'll take a deeper look at the sports conversation with a Yankee fan focusing on which arguments to avoid altogether because you simply can't win. Not that winning is everything, but to some, it's the difference between a thought-provoking debate and a waste of time. These arguments can be categorized into three types, (as we're wont to do): *Comparative, superlative,* and *hypothetical.*

Now, don't get us wrong, we're not singling out Yankee fans here as the only ones who take part in these arguments. They've been a part of the sports lexicon for years. Could the '85 Bears have beaten the '79 Steelers? Who is the all-time greatest hockey goalie? If Karl Malone were healthy, would the Lakers have beaten the Pistons in the 2004 NBA Championship?

These conversations are the stuff that entire sports feature series are made of. Not to say that these conversations aren't fun. You can go on for hours about a plethora of subjects impressing people with a wealth of knowledge. But if you're looking to lay down the law on a Yankee fan, an argument based without fact or truth is NOT the way to go. They'll say anything they want, no matter how crazy, and really can't be *proven* wrong.

COMPARATIVE

Take two of anything and compare them. There are so many subjective factors and variables involved that it's virtually impossible to formulate a solid conclusion, no matter how hard you try. Yet, Yankee fans perpetually have an arsenal of rootin'-tootin' doozies at the ready to drive you to the brink of insanity. Here's one they like:

"Derek Jeter has more postseason hits than anyone in baseball history."

Sure, given that his team is in the postseason every year thanks to the current salary system (SEE: Chapter Eleven) and add to that the fact that there are more rounds in the playoffs thanks to the wild-card set-up. That allows Jeter more opportunities than anyone besides he, Jorge Posada, and Bernie Williams has. But would Yankee fans mention that? A shake of our Magic eight-ball says, "All signs point to no."

> The dumbest thing anyone ever said to me was that 'Joe DiMaggio was better than Ted Williams because he had a fifty-six-game hitting streak and won as many MVPs.
>
> — *Matt Kennedy*

Really? Hmmm, well couldn't you just as easily tweak that to say "Ted Williams was better than Joe DiMaggio because he once hit .406 and won as many MVPs?" But then you just wind up sparring back and forth like Tyson and Holyfield. Look, we know you really want to refute their *yankiotic* statements and hit 'em with numbers, slay 'em with stats, and perhaps even bite their ear off. Fine. Here you go:

	Yrs	G	AB	R	H	2B	3B	HR	RBI	BB	SO	BA	OBP	SLG	SB	CS
Ted Williams	'39–'52	1427	5096	1275	1767	366	62	324	1264	1329	444	.347	.484	.634	20	14
Joe DiMaggio	'36–'48	1405	5609	1146	1853	320	111	303	1277	594	282	.330	.398	.589	30	8

This comparison shows a similar number of games for both of them, from the beginning of their careers through age thirty-three. Not that this should be news to anyone, but Teddy Ballgame was the better hitter. Yes, he struck out more and had fewer stolen bases and triples, but c'mon. Joltin' Joe was pretty darn good in his own right, and the slightly better fielder to boot.

	Pos	G	PO	A	E	DP	FP	lgFP	RFg	lgRFg	LF	CF	RF
Ted Williams	OF	2152	4158	142	113	30	.974	.977	2.00	2.21	1984	0	169
Joe DiMaggio	OF	1722	4529	153	105	30	.978	.974	2.72	2.31	66	1638	18

Who's to say why the Yankee Clipper had more putouts in fewer games? Maybe Williams played with more strikeout pitchers, maybe the wind swirled to centerfield more in Yankee Stadium, maybe DiMaggio had a magnet with an opposing charge in the ball causing it to fly to him. Who knows? Who cares?

Former All-Star pitcher Jack Morris has been quoted as saying, "Most people believe Babe Ruth was the greatest player ever. I wonder if he could hit a split-finger fastball." The point is, you'll never know. With all the facts, Yankee fans will still try to pull a trump card and tell you that Joe DiMaggio had more championship rings than Ted Williams; hence, he was the better player.

The last we checked, there were nine men on the field at one time and even if you're the unanimous MVP, without a supporting cast, you're not going to win. Ask Barry Bonds. If this were tennis, we could make the case that Pete Sampras was better than Yannick Noah because he has won more major tournaments. But we could also make the case that Yannick Noah had a cooler name. And our point of all this is a resounding . . . So what? This is why comparing gets you nowhere. They're both Hall of Famers who'll forever be synonymous with the word "baseball." Is it really worth chomping an ear off?

FUN FACT:

Thirty-six percent of all Yankee fans acquire their baseball knowledge from beer commercials.

Past vs. present

It is much easier to compare players or teams in the same era rather than different eras. That is a nearly impossible task. However, Yankee fans love pushing the envelope by comparing different teams from different eras in different sports.

"The Yankees dynasties were better than the dynasties in other organized sports."

Right? Well, as all comparative arguments are, it's tough to say, but the *Wall Street Journal* (2/11/05) came up with an index to answer just such a question. In looking at the most dominant dynasties of all-time, they, naturally, wound up focusing on the Montreal Canadians in hockey, the Boston Celtics in basketball, and the Yankees in baseball.

Here's a unique approach with which to force-feed them: The Yankees have twenty-six World Series titles to the Red Sox six, for a greater than four:one ratio. Meanwhile, the Celtics have sixteen championships to the Knicks two, a ratio of eight:one. (We're sorry, we were hoping not to drop mathematics on you, but we felt it necessary to illustrate our point.) Of course, Yankee fans are quick to note that there were fewer teams in the league when the Celtics won. But in the *Wall Street Journal's* "dynasty index" for all championship teams in North American sports history went even further. By their figuring, the 1957–1969 Celtics, have a higher *index* than do the '47–'62 Yankees. If this debate was a game of "Rock, paper, scissors", then you can see Boston's eleven titles in thirteen years is paper to New York's rock of ten titles in sixteen years. (At this point, Yankee fans will admit to not considering basketball a sport.)

After drubbing them with that barrage of sports lore, you've left the Yankee fan very little breathing room in their argument. Rather than surrender, they regularly take the "Yankee way" out and deny allegiance to other sports. One such diplomatic fan, Alan Cahill from Queens, after running out of ammo retreated to, "Nobody even cares about basketball, football, or hockey anyway. Baseball is the only sport that counts."

However, if the Knicks are doing well . . .

> I'm always amazed how they'll bring up their ring count (if they don't win for the next ninety years, they'd still bring up twenty-six rings), but a team like Boston doesn't mention sixteen rings to Knick fans (unless some stupid New York fan brags about their "dominance" in the '90s) as Canadian fans don't constantly remind Bruin or Red Wing fans about their twenty-three rings.
>
> — *Greg Prince, Mets fan*

Are you dizzy yet? That's why it's called the Spin Zone. It's almost a deep-seeded sense of denial that corrupts them from realizing the truth. Imagine Yankee fans were as obnoxious as they are now, but hadn't been privy to twenty-six world championships.

Let's say they had only two. They'd still drive us to drink . . . more. It's not the number; it's what they do with that number. The fact that they root for a team that's earned (bought?) a championship twenty-six times gives Yankee fans a sense of entitlement they feel they deserve. But as Greg elaborated, Celtics fans or Canadiens fans don't cling to that same entitlement.

Be wary of the: "What have you done lately" angle

Continuing with the point of Yankee hypocrisy, it's not really a comparative concept, but Yankee fans love to play whichever side of the fence gains them greater bragging rights. If their team is doing well, it's all about being "in the now." But should their team not be so good *at that time,* "heh, fuggedaboudit!" They got twenty-six championships in the can that say they don't give a rat's heiney about what's currently happening.

You, however, are bound by whichever rules they allot you. If the Yankees are down, you're not allowed to poke fun because they revert to their favorite number—twenty-six, the celebration of all those past championships. But should they be in the lead, they won't hesitate to let you have it.

The following is an actual conversation with Jonathan Sroka, the institute's director of research, in September 2005 as the Red Sox were a game behind NY going into the final weekend of the season after leading for much of the year.

> YANKEE FAN: I can't wait for the playoffs to start so the Yankees can add to their twenty-six championships.

> JS: I'm a Red Sox fan.

> YANKEE FAN: Oh, hey, sorry you guys choked again.

> JS: Actually, they didn't choke last year [2004].

YANKEE FAN: Geez, typical Sox fan always bringing up the past.

As we said, their hypocrisy is stunning.

Be careful though with these games as you're only on even ground if their team has failing. If they have the past AND the present angle, they'll make your life miserable.

Like a good chess player, they can seal off any escape for you. If you try to switch the subject to another sport—BAM!—"Other sports don't matter." If you bring up the past —BAP!—"Quit living in the past!" If you bring up the present —BANG!—"We've got twenty-six championships. And you losers only have [insert number lesser than twenty-six]!" CHECKMATE! (Forget en passant, they've got "le standard doble" or "double standard.")

SUPERLATIVE

In high school, these were a little easier to pin down—"best student." This was the person who studied hard and got all the right answers. There was a thin pool to choose from and they all were being judged on the same scale, from the same curriculum by many of the same teachers, etc. Or "best dressed." These fashion magnates didn't follow the trends; they set them. But the one deemed "best dressed" was done so based on one prevailing fashion trend or "look" at the time. Try determining the "best dressed" in the *history* of your school. It's hard to say—unless Tommy Hilfiger was an alum.

Here are two superlative arguments you'll likely encounter if you get stuck speaking with a Yankee fan for more than three minutes:

In 1998, I argued with a Yankee fan who said there was no doubt that Joe Torre was the greatest manager EVER. I, of course, disagreed using Torre's many past failures and maintained he wasn't even the best manager of the day, whom I believed was Felipe Alou, who was working miracles with the Expos with way less money and talent.

— *B.J. Cook*

A Yankee fan once told me that Don Mattingly was the greatest player in history. I just shook my head and said, "Right, and I suppose Don Larsen should be in the Hall of Fame just because he pitched *one* perfect game in 1956."

— *Todd Link*

If they want to think that Don Mattingly was the greatest player ever, let them go home, drink from their Don Mattingly souvenir mug, sleep with their Don Mattingly bobblehead, and play "Don Mattingly John Madden Football" for all you care. More power to 'em if that's what makes 'em happy.

As we mentioned, even Babe Ruth can't be compared to today's sluggers. With the fences moved in, the use of "the juice," diluted pitching, the DH, etc., there are too many variables to accurately and decisively go there.

Abner Doubleday suggests . . . Never accompanying a Yankee fan to a sports bar or an archery range.

Oh, and just know Yankee fans are in love with Joe Torre. He is their god. Sleep in the same room with a Yankee fan and they mumble his name in their sleep. His name surfaces in both comparative and superlative arguments. Not that he's a bad manager, but this is where you have all the circumstantial evidence on your side, yet will not be able to get a Yankee fan to budge on this one.

Joe Torre is still the best manager in baseball today. Everyone says he's got so much talent, but what he's done with that talent, the egos, and the injuries over the past few years is amazing. He's also player friendly, but doesn't take any crap either. He smells of lilacs all the time and if you pull on his ear, candy comes out of his bellybutton!

— *Derek Snow*

Okay, fine, so we added that last part about the lilacs and the bellybutton candy, but the rest is simply ridiculous. Mr. Snow recognizes the talent part, but injuries and egos aren't going to ruin the show for any manager when you have Yankee bucks to absorb any difficulties along the way. [See Chapter Eleven for the topic of money.] It plays such a huge part in the Joe Torre argument. If he is the greatest manager ever, why didn't he win before he was made a Sith for the evil empire? It's all right, though, New York Giants fans said the same thing about Bill Parcels until he stopped winning. Just let them have their fantasies about Joe Torre and his flowing golden hair and rippling bronzed torso.

The one thing you can't let them have is that topic that they have anointed "given" status to. Y'know what "given" status is. Donald Trump wears a hairpiece. Given. Lennox Lewis could beat the snot out of Gary Coleman. Given. Anna Kournikova would not have sex with us. Given. The 1998 Yankees were the greatest team of all time. Giv—WHOA!!! Who tried to slip that one in?!

Yankee fans will sneak this into conversation as often as a U.S. senator will slide a congressional pay raise into a bill about homeland defense. See if you can spot their ruse:

> I graduated from Rutgers University with a Bachelors of Communications and a concentration in public relations in 1998, the same year the Yankees had the greatest team ever. Though my concentration was in public relations, I ended up getting a job as a copywriter for an advertising firm.

"The Greatest Team Ever." That's a bold statement. And they don't even leave it open for debate. Their knowledge of baseball (1996–present for the majority of them) can't even begin to understand what they're saying. The Cubs had some pretty darn good teams in the early part of the twentieth century. And what of Mantle's Yankees? Or the Big Red Machine? Or the A's dynasty of the '70s? I guess they don't count, right?

With such a changing game, it's impossible to make that statement for most reasonable people, but not for Yankee fans. The 1998 Yankees had a DH, a "live ball," diluted pitching thanks to the expansion era, perhaps some of the players were juiced; it's really hard to tell how that team would've fared against all the historical teams. And that's all you can really do with that topic. Explain the difficulty in qualifying their accomplishments against the other great teams and if they continue to press their opinion, cock your head to the side and look at them as a dog would if you tried explaining to him the Theory of Relativity. You might want to add a bark for effect.

HYPOTHETICAL

The cornerstone of any sports fan's arsenal. It's really the only thing that keeps people sane through the bad times. And no one does this better than a Yankee fan.

Steve Bartman, "the Tuck Rule," the "Music City Miracle,"—all have become familiar references in this type of argument. "Well, we WOULDA won IF . . . " This one should make you laugh. Take the previous example about Karl Malone. If he weren't injured, the Lakers would've humiliated the woeful Pistons. Yes, and if the Hawks didn't lose far more games than anyone else, *they* would've beaten the Pistons. And if we weren't stuck behind this computer writing this book and had an ounce of athletic ability, perhaps our fathers would've been proud enough to show up at parent's weekend that one lonely autumn. Woulda shoulda coulda. Blah blah blah.

There are so many possible combinations of hypothetical arguments; we couldn't possibly list them all. But just try to realize that any thought a Yankee fan could dream up, no matter how outrageous, you should expect them to say it . . . loudly and often. You won't ever like it but, at least, you'll be prepared when it inevitably happens.

And that was the Spin Zone. Wasn't that fun? Please take all your belongings and exit to the right of the car. Barf bags are available near the cotton candy vendor. (Just don't ask him for a cotton candy. He serves it to you by pulling on Joe Torre's ear.)

Abner Doubleday suggests . . . Stop letting Yankee fans make Bucky f@*#&' Dent a f@*#&' folk hero.

THE MYTH—A.K.A. "FAHRENHEIT 1978":

According to the deluded masses:

"Bucky f@*#&' Dent hit a game-winning three-run homer in the ninth off Mike Torrez. Yanks go on to win the World Series."

Those with a better memory would add a few stats to flavor the saga:

"And that little' &#*% only hit four dingas all season!"

Even Tommy Lasorda once quipped, "He couldn't hit water if he fell out of a f%*@#&' boat!" Basically, we all remember Bucky Dent for crushing Boston's hopes in yet another season. But did Bucky actually, single-handedly; beat the Red Sox with a blistering shot that still resonates all throughout the Fens?

The Fact: As is the case with much great folklore, the tale grew taller as time passed and the truth became fabled. Dent's three run blast DID NOT, we repeat, DID NOT win the American League East Division tie-breaking game. Down 2-0 going into the seventh, the Yanks started a two-out rally when Chris Chambliss and Roy White singled. Then Dent, a .243 hitter, came to the plate and swatted a 1-1 pitch inches over the Green Monster giving the Yanks a 3–2 lead. (Shortly thereafter, then Sox manager and future Pedro Martinez sparring partner, Don Zimmer, created the moniker, "Bucky f@*#&' Dent."

The final score was 5–4. Do the math . . . there was obviously a lot more action from both sides following Dent's dinger. Both the Red Sox and Yankees scored two mores runs. The final and winning run came in the top of the eight off the bat of "Mr. October" himself . . . Reggie Jackson. His solo blast would be *the* one run the Yanks would need to prevail. The Sox still had a chance to score in the bottom of the ninth with two out and two on but Goose Gossage got Yaz to pop out to left.

And Bucky f@*#&' Dent went on to become a legend in baseball history without actually winning the game. Were it not for this infamous homer, he surely would've disappeared into the annals of the *Baseball Register Stat Book*. At best, he would've been a trivia question on *Jeopardy*. Meanwhile, Reggie Jackson went on to have a candy bar named after him. Ironically, it contained the exact same ingredients as the Baby Ruth.

CHAPTER TEN—
MAKING YANKEE FRIENDS AND
INFLUENCING YANKEE PEOPLE

With all these obstacles toward civil and non-antagonistic communication, one might wonder how a friendship could ever be forged with the fanatics. Can you hang out with a Yankee fan? We've received myriad statements ranging along the spectrum from "No" to "not a chance" to "no way" all the way down to "I'd rather make love to a bee hive."

But let us assure you; with a little bit of honey and some patience, it can be done.

ENTERTAINING YANKEE FANS

Let's say you're having a backyard barbecue. The summer months beckon you to the grill. The strategically placed citronella candles act as an invisible barrier between your party and bugs. However, some determined mosquitoes manage to get past your defenses and threaten to mar the festivities. They are no ordinary bugs, but loud, relentless mashers who prey on the contentedness and docile qualities of their hosts. They are rabid insects resilient to common pesticides found in most drug stores such as "Deep Woods Off" or the stronger version, "Fuck Off." They are, after all, Yankee fans.

Don't let them smell failure. They wear navy blue and white T-shirts and caps emblazoned with an "N" nestled cozily over a "Y." Whereas most bugs hover around the trash, these creatures *spew* trash from their mouths in the form of moronic rantings. Yet even the bugs know better to avoid them, preferring the aroma of rotten eggs and soiled diapers to that of the common Yankee fan.

We all have friends who are Yankee fans or know someone who does. They're everywhere. They multiply like Starbucks franchises. They come out of the woodwork between April and October, especially if their team is doing well. And somehow, much like the aforementioned aphids, they always wind up at your neighbor's Labor Day weekend block party.

- Don't let them deter you from your fun. Entertaining Yankee fans is not as dire a situation as you may deem it. All you need to know are these easy tips and you won't even know they're there.
- Don't wear any clothing that represents any sports team other than the Yankees.
- Don't wear any clothing that highlights accomplishments of other sports teams.
- Don't expose any part of the skin that has a tattoo or mole in the shape of another sports team's logo. Make sure clothing covers all suspect areas.
- Don't wear any clothing at all.
- In fact, you may want to skip the cookout altogether. After all, you and your neighbor aren't that close anyway and besides, they're showing a *Godfather* marathon on the Spike Network.

Sorry, we aren't going to let you take the easy way out this time. It's your summer and you deserve an enjoyable afternoon, so that is what you shall be granted. Just be prepared for some verbal combat. And it always starts with them.

Let's say the team depicted on your jersey happens to be out-performing the Yankees at that particular point in time, it doesn't matter; they'll still talk smack. The first thing they try to do is berate your team, your town, the people in your town, and the mayor of your town, whom they'll refer to as "the Mayor of Shitsville."

That's okay. Just let it go because this will be about as harmless as it will get. Merely try to keep the conversation light and fun. No talk about the trade deadline, championship teams in any sports, celebrities who've been seen with Derek Jeter, etc.

You may ask us, "But what if we're having a good time and someone asks to watch the game?" You should render every media outlet in the house non-functional. If they even find out a score, it could send the party into a tailspin. You may ask how could this happen? Well, if they lose, they'll pout like a four-year-old whose hand was caught in the cookie jar. God forbid they're on a losing streak of two in a row. You'll have to talk them off a ledge (or push them off) only to have their depression recreate itself as rage towards all other fans.

If this doesn't work (and odds are it won't) you may be in need of the "advanced course" of Yankee fan management. Remember: barbeque = fun. This is not the time to unleash a Class III or IV on them. As infuriating as it may be, let them have their theories and don't let them interfere with your enjoyment.

You might ask, "How is that possible?" As far-fetched as the idea might sound, there is a way to befriend a Yankee fan for the afternoon or during your time in the same vicinity. You have to enter an almost zen-like state, but you can do so with a little focus and some tricks we're going to tell you. Practice them before social gatherings and it will become second nature to you.

First, a key in allowing a Yankee fan into your life is to understand their dogmatic system of belief. The Yankee zealots believe very deeply in ten very basic rules:

TEN COMMANDMENTS OF BEING A YANKEE FAN

1. Thou shall not have other baseball gods before Me for I am the Lord, thy Steinbrenner, who brought you, the chosen ones, out of the land called Yonkers and unto the Bronx.
2. Thou shall not take the name of thy LORD, your God, in vain. Examples: "That f*#%'n Steinbrenner!" or "Jesus, Mary, and Steinbrenner!"
3. Remember to keep holy the Sabbath Game Day. (That goes double for all post season games)
4. Honor your father and your mother . . . unless they won't let you attend games at Yankee Stadium.
5. Thou shall not kill . . . a Red Sox or Mets fan unless you are sure you can get away with it.
6. Thou shall not commit adultery . . . with any current or former wife of Jose Canseco.
7. Thou shall not steal . . . signs from the opposing team until at least the third inning.
8. Thou shall not bear false witness against your neighbor . . . unless you stand to benefit from said testimony.
9. Thou shall not interfere with any ball in play unless it will help the Yankees and dramatically change the outcome of the game, and/or series.
10. Thou shall not covet thy neighbor's ballpark, for it is nowhere near as nice as the bastion of Yankee worship; "*thy* Stadium."

These rules are tantamount to their allegiance; should they break any of them, they must say twelve "Hail Yogis," four "Our Steinbrenners," and recite Lou Gehrig's speech twice. Do not forsake their ten commandments . . . at least, not at the barbecue.

Remember, during your resignation to allow them their peace, do NOT pester them. They are prone to outbursts so if you see them getting worked up preparing for a *tête-à-tête*, move on to the next topic. Stick and move, stick and move.

Here are some tricks to learn when you don't want to properly engage your counterparts:

Be understanding—Take into account where they are coming from. There is some truth to what they say, *i.e.* if they say, "Yankee Stadium is the greatest stadium ever built," the truth is that Yankee Stadium is, IN FACT, a stadium, NOT a movie theater or a sky-scraper or a space station. So you should look at the heart of the matter, the basic premise of their argument and go from there. If they get two out of three of the words correct as in "Stadium" and "Yankee," but misfire on the word "greatest," then give them an "A" for effort.

Be self-effacing—Prepare to poke fun at yourself. It will lighten the mood and it may even allow them to make some much-needed concessions.

"I actually put money down on the Devil Rays to take the division this year. Boy, what was I thinking?"

Nod and smile—Make them think you're actually listening to them. If they laugh, you laugh. Hum "The Girl from Ipanema" in your head as they speak, just be ready for a change in subject or a question. If he catches you dozing, you may be busted. (This also works at company parties.)

If you know a secret, keep it to yourself—"They're wrong," you say to yourself. "The Yankees did not have a lower payroll than the Mets in the summer of 2000." But do you tell them? It's silly to cut them off while they're on a roll. Let them speak while you keep a mental list of the mistakes they make (it's okay to enter the data on a piece of scrap paper or your palm pilot if there are too many mis-takes to remember), and then proceed cautiously.

Ignore them—As we just mentioned, stick and move. The only difference from simply refraining from going on the offensive is that now, not only do you not push the offense; you take your field off the team. You don't even acknowledge any comment they make.

YANKEE FAN: "Yankee fans are the best in the world."

YOU: "Say . . . that really is an interesting butterfly. I wonder how long its gestation period is."

No matter how much his statement irks you, let it go. The high road, take the high road (and if you have to be high to take the high road, so be it). Again, do NOT pester them by cutting them off in mid-sentence, screaming, "Ooooo buddy, you're soooo wrong, and here's why . . . !" Your time will come.

After you've gained their trust, you can consult your trusty note pad and start unwinding their tangled logic. Begin with a statement indicating that a well-thought out debate is about to take place.

Y'know, I've been thinking about what you said . . .

Then add a phrase praising the reasoning behind their claim.

Y'know, I've been thinking about what you said; *a very smartly-conceived point, I might add, about . . .*

Make sure you correctly title the topic as "pro-Yankee" and not "anti-." For instance, terming it "the Yankees' complete disregard for a competitive balance" will get you nowhere whereas rephrasing it as "other teams' inability to keep up with the Yankees" would.

Y'know, I've been thinking about what you said; a very smartly-conceived point, I might add, about *other teams' inability to keep up with the Yankees' spending.*

It is at this point that you can ease your way into drilling holes into his theory, while making it seem that the argument is merely an extension of his belief. We call this the old "yes, but . . . " tactic. Agree and then contradict. Observe:

Y'know, I've been thinking about that thing you said; a very smartly-conceived point, I might add, about other teams' inability to keep up with the Yankees' spending. *As you claimed, since there is no salary cap, other teams are free to spend as much as they want. That's true, but . . . without the revenue coming in, they'll go bankrupt trying to keep up with New York.*

And for the "you moronic douche bag," part that you're dying to add on to the end of your statement, remember to use your "inner voice" so as not to undo any good feelings you've fostered. Then when he comes back at you with more rhetoric, revert back to –

Say, . . . that really is an interesting butterfly. I wonder how long its gestation period is.

Just say your point once. Do not repeat points or it will look like you are badgering. Do NOT antagonize. It's like drinking a big glass of milk in front of a lactose-intolerant person. We believe it was Immanuel Kant who said, "When opening the door to a whole new way of looking at the world, one must use the gloves of the lion cub." (Again, we have to check the validity of this.) The slightest sign that you're confronting them and you're back to square one.

If you go into the "yes, but" defense too quickly, you could injure a groin and get yourself placed on the fifteen-day disabled list. This method is a gentle way to fine-tune their thesis into one that is more accurate. How can they feel antagonized by someone who speaks so eloquently?

Posing questions is dangerous as well. Although harmless on the surface, it could damage the rapport you've worked hard to establish. Even if you're curious about Yankee history, if you ask them a question that only a true, life-long Yankee fan would be able to answer, they might end up wriggling in anguish trying to come up with a feasible excuse for not knowing the answer. But watch out, as they'll often somehow manage to throw it back in your face. Take this example:

> YOU: How many more at bats did Maris have than Mantle when he broke the Babe's single season home run record in '61?*
>
> YANKEE FAN: Ahem, I was very young then and um, spent most of the summer, um, in the hospital with a bout of, uh . . . uh-cute spina bifida. Sure, that's it. And even though I made a full recovery, I've tried to erase the whole emotionally scarred summer from my mind. The memories are just too painful. But thanks for bringing it up, you heartless jackass.

*Maris had 108 more at-bats including thirty-two more walks.

Okay, you've made it this far. You're now ready to go back to the barbeque and put some of your schooling to the test. Before you go, take a look at the chart depicted below, as it will provide a good jumping off point for your impending reunion with the Yankee fan. These are some common antagonistic phrases that can easily be modified to appear more amenable to the Yankee fan.

ENGLISH–TO–YANKEE FAN CONVERSION CHART

Wrong way to phrase it	Correct way to phrase it
Steinbrenner just buys his teams.	It's a shame how other owners are just too cheap and obviously don't care if they win.
Most Yankee fans are merely band-wagon-jumpers who equate their own self worth with the success of the team.	The Yankees, America's eternal sweetheart, simply have a bigger fan base than any other team.
Yankee Fans aren't real fans.	It must be great to only have to follow a team when they're winning. I bet that sure saves a lot of heartache.
Yankee Stadium is a rat-infested shit-hole.	Beauty, thy name is Yankee Stadium.
Mickey Mantle was a raging alcoholic who never knew when to quit.	Mickey Mantle was not a quitter!
Ted Williams was a far better player than Joe DiMaggio.	Imagine how many more World Series titles the Yanks would have if they had Ted Williams?
How much do the Yankees pay the umps to give them ALL of the calls?	It must give you unconditional assurance knowing that there is one set of rules for the Yankees and a completely different set of rules for everyone else.
It is truly amazing how badly the Yankees choked in the 2004 ALCS.	It is truly amazing how compassionate & sportsman-like the Yankees were by letting the lowly Red Sox win the 2004 ALCS.
Yankees Suck!	It is unfortunate that due to inflated payrolls and lack of an adequate salary cap, small-market teams have a difficult time competing with the great Yankees
You are talking out of your ass!	I see that you are bi-lingual . . . and flexible.
Go f*** yourself!	Would you like to borrow a hand towel and some ointment?
George Steinbrenner is a voracious, deplorable, egomaniacal windbag.	George Steinbrenner is a *fat*, voracious, deplorable, egomaniacal windbag.

HOW TO TALK TO A YANKEE FAN CO-WORKER
(Bringing sports politics to the office)

So . . . you are plagued with the unfortunate situation of having to work with a Yankee fan. Assuming you are a "nine-to-fiver," that means you have to suffer them no less than forty hours a week, or roughly fifty percent of your waking life. We truly sympathize with you. But what do you do? Well, let's see what we've learned so far with this pop quiz. Get out your pencils . . . To successfully deal with a Yankee fan co-worker you:

A. Find a middle ground so you can tolerate them.
B. Get another job.
C. Report their "tax write-offs" to the IRS.
D. Slash their tires in the parking garage during your lunch break.
E. None of the above.

We know options C and D seem like the obvious choices but we here at the *How to Talk to a Yankee Fan Institute* cannot condone such behavior (in print). And while choice B is certainly a quick fix, the difficulty of relocating renders it rather unfeasible. So, we'll bite the bullet, take the high road, and walk you through option A.

WATER COOLER TACTICS

In a white-collar environment**, a Yankee fan isn't likely to start anything, as it would not fit in with proper office etiquette. In fact, they may appear to be more friendly or sympathetic than usual when their team is doing well. Don't be fooled by their intentions, though. They'll play it safe with statements like, "Boy, that A-Rod is on fire. It looks like he's finally adjusted to the New York environment," and "Tough break on that call at first yesterday. I thought your guys had it." But this manner of rubbing it in is considered "ethical" and is technically not covered under harassment law. (Now if you were a foreign-speaking elderly female midget with a speech impediment and a prosthetic leg, you might have a case.)

Always expect the frequency of baseball conversations to be in direct relation to the size of the Yankees' division lead and subsequent success through the playoffs. (*i.e.* If the Yanks are doing well, that's all they want to discuss. If they are choking, there are "more important" things to worry about.)

Office cubicles are generally safe ground, but still, be wary if the Yanks are flying high. Don't go to their court. E-mail any important documents from at least four cubicles away. (If you are less than four cubicles away, he can say, "Heh heh, can't drop the memo off in person? You're as lazy as Manny Ramirez running out that fly ball last night. Heh heh.")

As much as you want to, resist the urge to vandalize any Yankee articles, pictures, or other merchandise that might be tacked up on their cubicle wall. It's too dangerous and someone might see you. If you absolutely MUST deface it, sneak off to the copy room and smudge your hands with toner. Then go over and innocently fawn over his paraphernalia. Chances are it will lose all sentimental and face value with your palm prints on it. But again, we don't condone this (in print).

WHEN THEY LOSE

Let's say the Yanks just lost an important series. (Yeah, we're aware those occurrences are as rare as Paris Hilton getting a "headache," but we're speaking hypothetically here.) You know you want to bring up the game. But as we've learned, you're better off with small talk, something pedestrian like, "working hard, or hardly working?" However, by saying that particular overused cornball phrase, you run a larger risk of getting stabbed with a pair of rusty scissors than you would by referencing the recent sports contest. Anyway, keep it simple and try a little back-door chicanery to lure *them* into bringing it up first. You can set the bait by asking them a question to "innocently" force their hand.

> YOU: Hey, did you see the final episode of *American Idol* last night? Man, that Carrie Underwood is hot! Gimme five minutes with her and—
>
> YANKEE FAN: What the hell is wrong with you? You know the deciding game was on, you buffoon!
>
> YOU: Oh right, I forgot. What happened?
>
> YANKEE FAN: Like you don't know.
>
> YOU: I don't, actually. My kids are addicted to *Idol* so I got stuck watching that. I take it things didn't fare well for the Bombers?
>
> YANKEE FAN: If we weren't at work right now I'd, I'd—

At this point, he'll be so incensed that you could actually take his pulse just by looking at the veins jutting out of his forehead. If you do, count to yourself and don't stare! Otherwise, take our earlier advice and "stick and move." Just fake an important meeting with the boss and politely excuse yourself. Remember, he has those rusty scissors.

WHEN THEY LOSE TO YOUR TEAM

If it happened to be *your* team that bested the Yanks and you just *gotta* rub it in, always let him make the first move. Treat the day like any other day with banal salutations and idiotic chitchat. Remember, Yankee fans always handle defeats in one of three ways:

1. They shrug it off and pretend to be unfazed by the loss. This will be followed by constant reminders of their past successes. (Read: "twenty-six and counting . . . ")
2. They'll use every excuse in the book as to why the loss occurred.

3. Complete avoidance.

You can see what their reaction will be by heading towards his cubicle/office. Don't make eye contact. As you get closer, veer off course and visit someone else. If he remains in place, you can expect him to approach you before the workday has ended. If your arrival in the vicinity causes him to flee, don't expect a congratulatory gesture anytime soon. In that event, spend the rest of the day visiting his cubicular neighbors.

In all probability, don't expect them in the office the next day. But it's NOT because they can't take the heat. No, they'll always have a "rock solid excuse."

FUN FACT:

Studies show that only three out of eight Yankee fans show up for work the day after their team is humiliated.

TOP TEN MOST COMMON YANKEE FAN EXCUSES FOR AVOIDANCE

1. My kid came down with a bout of scurvy.
2. Did your power go out too? My alarm was disabled.
3. My pipes burst and there was water everywhere. At that point, I decided to work from home.
4. I converted religions and was busy accepting Jesus Christ as my personal savior.
5. I was traveling for work. Dammit, I would've rather been at the office though. (Be wary if the janitor uses this one.)
6. I got dysentery from eating some bad Indian food last night.
7. I pulled a hammy on the treadmill yesterday. I had to spend the day laid up in bed.
8. I popped a couple Viagara thinking they were Tums and then, well . . . you do the math.

9. My stigmata was acting up and I didn't want to bleed all over the office.
10. How can you even think about baseball with the big project coming up? Get your priorities straight, man.

Only a Yankee fan would be arrogant (there's that word again) enough to think those excuses might work. But don't go trying it yourself should your team flounder or they'll have ammunition to use against you in the future. You have to bite the bullet and show up. If anything gets out of hand, human resources can get involved. However, there's a problem if human resources is the one causing the problem. And if it's your boss, let it go. It's hard to put your resume on monster.com while you're clubbing him to death with a computer keyboard.

**If you work in a blue-collar work environment, we can't help you. You are screwed. Any confrontation with a Yankee fan will find you on the opposite end of a severe thrashing from a two-by-four, pipe wrench, or the closest makeshift weapon available at the job site. Our only advice; go back to pretending you don't speak English.

HOW TO TALK TO A YANKEE FAN YOU'RE MARRIED TO

There is a major difference in simply entertaining a Yankee fan for the afternoon and spending the majority of your life with one. Those immortal words, "I do . . . " accompanied by the vows you took, dictate that you must stand by their side "though sickness and in health, for richer or poorer, in good times and in bad . . . " But when you've trod the aisle with a Yankee fan, that pledge must also include, "through steroid abuse and humiliation, inflated salaries and deals past the trade deadline, and in World Series winning streaks and utter collapse(s) of overpriced superstars." Unfortunately, you no longer have the standard escape hatch of; "Welp, it's gettin' late. Guess I gotta be gettin' home to feed the dog."

Similar to a mixed marriage, *interfanatic* couples often deal with bigots who point fingers and talk behind their backs. Ultimately the couples prevail, and wear it as a badge of honor; something they've overcome together. But if you're an Orioles fan and your spouse is a Yankees fan, then, come game day,—IT'S ON! You'll be the ones pointing fingers and talking behind each other's back.

Abner Doubleday suggests . . . Sitting Yankee fans at a "Yankee Fan Only" table at weddings.

Like with many relationships, the first few months are idyllic. At the onset of an interfanatical marriage, a ballgame could be on in the background and you'd be so completely lost in your mate's eyes you wouldn't even glance twice at it. Perhaps your spouse even wears a Yankee hat on your Polynesian honeymoon simply to tell the natives, "Hey, guess what everybody? We're from New York."

Eventually, the couple reaches the juncture where "farting in front of each other" is the primary method of communication. One day the Yankee game will be on; he'll feign interest, watching with one eye, while she fixates on the TV as if it were a crystal ball. There's a tense moment and the Yankees lose out on a close call. She is livid. He is trying to contain his glee. They utter their first words to each other all day:

> SHE: Can you believe that garbage?! The umps just stole the game away from the Yankees.

> HE: Actually, I saw the whole play. It looked like a good call.

> SHE: I don't even know who you are anymore.

Any psychologist would tell you a spat like this indicates a much deeper, more severe problem in the relationship, something far beneath the surface of this paltry exchange. But, they'd be wrong.

This is the problem when interfanatical couples marry and the fireworks fade. In fact, it's the "love/hate the Yankees" relationship that keeps many a marriage on its toes.

SHE: Do these jeans make my ass look fat?

HE: No, pumpkin. It's the Yankee hat that does . . .

He'll laugh at his own joke. She won't. He'll explain, "C'mon, you gotta admit that was funny." She will eventually use this against him in a court of law.

DIVORCING A YANKEE FAN—MEN

Divorcing a Yankee fan may be tricky. There are usually only a few reasons divorce can be precipitated. "Irreconcilable differences" would be the primary choice here. Any self-respecting judge would expedite the process after learning that the defendant is a Yankee fan. "Temporary Insanity" is also a widely accepted alternative plea.

Problems commonly arise when it comes to "Distribution of Possessions." It is crucial for you to find a judge who is not a Yankee fan, otherwise you are sure to go home penniless with only the shirt on your back (which will be reclaimed after you have it laundered). She'll get to keep her things, your things, your kids' things, and things you didn't even know you had. But it's okay; you got out! Besides, what would you do with a bronzed imprint of Derek Jeter's butt anyway?

DIVORCING A YANKEE FAN—WOMEN

Always go with the "Domestic Violence" grounds, especially after the Yanks lose. Settle things in court too. Don't watch that Jennifer Lopez movie and think you can "take him." An angry Yankee fan is not someone you should mess with. That's a matter for the police.

Of course, to nip the possibility of violence in the bud, you can choose to support your spouse's Yankees. However, you will be the one who has to look at yourself in the mirror every day. You can always just withhold sex during the season—wait . . . that could be what caused this mess in the first place! Don't listen to us on this one. We're men fer cryin' out loud. What the hell do we know?

RAISED TO HATE

Be especially wary about what could happen if you have children in an interfanatical marriage. It's throwing a monkey wrench into an already damaged mechanism. There is a good chance there will be a custody battle even *without* a divorce. Having two children and thinking you can each mold one to your sports beliefs is just naïve. You'll only turn more passive-aggressive toward each other.

> JUNIOR: What's for dinner, mom?
>
> MOM: I'm ordering take out from Mickey Mantle's restaurant. The food is almost as good as "The Mick" was a ballplayer.

Or:

> JUNIOR: Hey dad, can you help me with my math homework?
>
> DAD: Sure, son. Take twenty-two championships; add four, and you have the number of championships the Yankees have won. If you follow your mom's team, you'd only be able to count to five.

That only precipitates a breakdown of all communication once the other party becomes aware of what is being taught.

> JUNIOR: Mommy, why aren't you and Daddy speaking?

MOM: Because sweetie, your Daddy is an arrogant prick.

This is not an acceptable response, unless you have raised a *Friggin' Ute*. Then, you can say whatever comes to mind. As for the other scenarios depicted in this chapter, we hope you study them, commit them to memory, and, for the love of God and all things Holy, do not stray from them when you find yourself in times of trouble.

TAKE ME OUT TO THE DOG PARK . . .

Hey, let's not leave animals out of the equation. You can identify an animal owned by a Yankee fan nearly as fast as you can identify its owner's allegiance. The next time you're walking through the park and hear the painful wail of a dogfight, stop and take a look at the participants: The one with the stream of foam cascading from its mouth will be a Rottweiler named Thor. The one that's whimpering while lying in a heap is a Cocker Spaniel named Truckee. Guess which canine belongs to the Yankee fan?

As the saying goes . . . "The apple doesn't fall far from the tree."—so describes the relationship between the Yankee fan and their pets. The most common domestic ones owned by Yankee fans are various breeds of: doberman pincer, pit bull, rottweiler, boa constrictor, betta splenden (fighting fish), electric eel, fire ant, tarantula, muskrat, and gerbil.

FUN FACT:

In 1983, while vacationing in Paraguay, George Steinbrenner bit a stray armadillo that wandered onto his patio. The armadillo died three days later. It now rests peacefully in George's Wild Game Hunting room.

CHAPTER ELEVEN—
MONEY TALKS

Mountains of logs have been sawed, milled, and packaged, then used—and recycled (the institute promotes environmentally-friendly practices)—in publishing opinions relating to the subject of payroll in the major leagues. The majority of pages are filled with rants on the Yankees unending quest to outspend most small, industrial nations countered with the integrity of these capitalistic endeavors.

We thought it befitting of Chapter Eleven to discuss the financing of the evil empire. After all, in order to keep up with the Yankees, that's exactly what every other major league team will eventually have to file for—Chapter Eleven. It's painfully obvious they don't pull any financial punches in their pursuit of excellence and George's frivolous shopping sprees are legendary. But we digress . . .

Nearly every single aspect of their annual payroll has already been discussed and dissected *ad nauseam* in books, magazines, periodicals, publications, and, most flawlessly, Letterman's monologue. However, it wasn't as Herculean a task as you'd think to find a different angle, a new weapon, if you will, to disarm any and all Kool-Aid drinkers who argue that the Yankees *only* have the highest payroll because they have the highest game attendance and network viewership, and that's *only* because they have the best fans, ya-da, ya-da, ya-*duh* . . .

Thanks in part to a grant from the SoSH Foundation, the *How to Talk to a Yankee Fan Institute* has funded the first comprehensive study on the impact money has on success in baseball. Before we dive into this topic, we thought we'd lay the foundation by getting a general sense of how fans around the league feel about the Yankees' own "Green Monster."

ARE THE YANKEES GOOD FOR BASEBALL?

Yes . . . they unite all other fans in their hatred.

— *Bill Abelson*

Yes because they have everything that you'd want for your team: an owner who wants to win so badly he'll spend an ungodly amount of money to buy players that you'd want on your team. And no, because they're like the United States picking on other little countries out there to steal what they want, like going to Iraq for oil or invading Arizona to take Randy Johnson.

— *Dustin Millman, flip-flopper*

No. They should move to Utah and become the Salt Basin Bombers. They should go away and leave New York to the Mets. The idea that baseball needs a dynasty or a big, bad team rubs my egalitarian impulses the wrong way. You can't force fans outside New York to not be Yankee fans but if they are (*and have only been since 1996*), they should receive some sort of electric shock every time the Yanks win just to make sure they're real fans.

— *Greg Prince*

Horrible! Baseball is a mess, and it all starts with the Yankees. They win with money and quite honestly, given their payroll, I would be embarrassed if I only had twenty-six rings to show for it. Their logo should be a picture of Gordon Gecko. Team motto: Greed is good. The pinstripes should be dollar signs. If everyone else would come along with me, I would never watch another game in my life.

— *Paul Nardizzi, author of* 602 Reasons to Be Pissed Off

Yes, it's like wrestling; you need a good bad guy or it's boring. Baseball without the Yankees would be like *Henry, Portrait of a Serial Killer*, without Henry.

— *Bill Burr, cast member,* Chapelle's Show

No, the Yankees are good for the Yankees.

— *Greg Faherty*

Yes, begrudgingly, I admit they're good for baseball as they represent Goliath to the many Davids that battle for preeminence every season. Furthermore, baseball is enjoying a level of popularity that extends across the globe. The Yanks have players from Japan and Latin American countries where baseball takes on a religious fervor. They broadcast games via satellite, Internet, and radio to a fan base far beyond our country's borders.

— *Sean Lambert*

Was Godzilla good for Japan?

— *Jimmy Dunn, author of* Funnyball

Once again, we see a nation divided. It appears difficult for some folks to put their personal feeling aside and opine objectively about the flaws in the current MLB wage wars. Conversely, no one is sicker of talking about their financial dominance than Yankee fans. They enjoy it about as much as the Vatican likes discussing the validity of The Dead Sea Scrolls. But surprisingly, there are sympathetic ears out there.

Dave Szpila, a Pirates fan (ouch) and radio personality from Albany, New York, sides with the poor Yanks. "Everyone else hates them but, let's face it; we'd all love to have a taste of their action.

What is George supposed to do? Bribe every other fan in America with a $300 check to buy their support? Most intelligent people saw right through that when the *other* George pulled that same scheme a few years back."

Frank DeFord, during his previously referenced lecture, was asked about the Yankees' spending. He put it nicely explaining that if you own a widget company, you're going to do all that you can trying to put all the other widget companies out of business. But in baseball, it can't work that way. That's why the government has granted an anti-trust exemption to baseball.

Imagine if the Yankees succeeded in putting all the other teams out of business. They wouldn't have any one left to play. (Of course, their fans would still be bragging that they won their seventy-third championship by forfeit and Derek Jeter III batted 1.000 for the series.)

Alas, that isn't the real issue with Yankee fans. As numbers begin to coagulate in a rabid Yankee fans' head, they dig themselves into a bottomless hole by adopting a stance grounded in stupidity. Their hubris comes to the forefront creating an obstacle toward their understanding simple macroeconomics.

"It's not the Yankees fault they spend;Any owner can do the same."

Adam Sivits was all over that one: "NO THEY CAN'T! Other teams don't sell merchandise in Prague. Other teams don't sign TV rights away for the small price of Japan's GDP. And other teams definitely can't pay $50 million in 'luxury' taxes. Use your head!"

Mets fan, Benjamin Hill, scoffed at this question. "Come on, the Expos used to broadcast their games through an elaborate network of tin cans and string. How much revenue do you suppose that brought in? They had to pack up and move to D.C. for cryin' out loud!"

Fellow Mets fan, AV was even less forgiving. "Right, and it wasn't the Nazis' fault that they were willing to commit genocide to try to take over the world; other countries could have tried the same thing."

Only Raj Nath seemed to come up with the most "far and balanced" solution. "Sure, other owners could easily do the same. All they have to do is get a huge network deal, a city with twenty million people, and unlimited funds. Piece of cake!"

This discourse allows us to segue smoothly into the real question at hand:

DO THE YANKEES JUST BUY THEIR TEAMS?

Most folks agreed with BJ Cook, who maintained, "Oh yeah, they definitely do. They've taken spending to an unprecedented level in professional sports and have all but eliminated at least four other teams before the season even starts."

The game of baseball, with all its quirks, makes a few million dollars negligible, but the tens of millions the Yankees overspend eliminate the possibility of letting fate decide the regular season for them. It's hard to find a gap in that logic considering they've made it to the post season ten years in a row and six of the last ten World Series.

Greg Prince agreed. "The Yankees actually buy two teams, one to field, one to have on deck should anything go wrong. All the other teams eventually have to make payroll decisions. The Yankees don't."

Our favorite southpaw, Bill Burr, rounds out this section with a definitive retort. "In the last five years that's exactly what they've done, and it's why they haven't won. That fathead Steinbrenner doesn't know how to put together a team. He just knows how to buy all the best players. I could do what he does. There's no science to it. People tend to forget that all those guys (Jeter, Rivera, etc.) came up through the farm system when GEORGE WAS SUSPENDED FROM BASEBALL!!! Today they just have a collection of great players, not a team."

Despite the fact that Yankee fans contend their payroll is only higher because they have more fans, hence higher game attendance and network viewership, they fail to mention *(or realize)* that the overall attendance in Yankee Stadium history is roughly seventy-two percent. *That is ten percent lower than the highest percentage in terms of lifetime capacity—Fenway Park.* Comparing the two teams shows that for the eighty-six years between Red Sox World Series victories, in which the Yankees won twenty-six, Boston still had a higher attendance percentage. Meanwhile, the Yankees have seen their lowest attendance numbers during their rare "drought years" and have only broken their own attendance numbers during championship years. Go figure . . .

DO OTHER TEAMS BUY THEIR TEAM JUST LIKE THE YANKEES?

Now the 1996 Yankees, they'll tell you, were chock full of homegrown players. But the fact is if you look at the forty-eight players who suited up for the big boys that year, you'll find that only nineteen of them were Yankee farmhands. And that includes September call-ups and minor role players. So doing the math (what, again with the damn math?!), you'll find that when they speak of their "homegrown" team, they're actually only speaking of thirty-nine percent of it. Hmm, doesn't sound like anything to brag about, does it? Especially when a team like the 2000 Twins out there who got plucked a whopping seventy-eight percent of their squad from their minor league system. Now that's what they call "the killer homegrown" or "Da kind club." Roll on, Minnesota! (*We apologize if that sounded a little gangsta.*)

New York, on the other hand, is on par with the 2001 As who, using the *Moneyball* strategy, built their team through trades mainly, only promoting forty percent themselves from down on the farm.

Yankee fans refuse to hear it. They jumped on the following Chicago White Sox fan:

> I don't talk to them anymore. Their stock comeback is "If it were your team buying players, you'd be happy." Yeah, you're right. And if I could fly and make myself invisible, that'd be swell too.
>
> — *Ken Blankstein, writer,* That 70s Show

Ken nailed this with a perfect dose of sarcasm. If his team could afford it, great. If another team could afford it, fantastic. If EVERY team could do it, then we're in business. But it's just WRONG that one team can do it. We suggest stapling the 2005 yearly payroll charts to a Yankee fan's face the next time they bring up this misguided point. Let's take it to the streets again to hear how the rest of the masses feel about this . . .

> No other team steals a player away at the last second just so another team can't have him. And no other team gives MLB the finger every year by laughing in the face of the payroll cap and subsequent luxury tax. So sure, the Sox and Angels may buy some players, but unlike the Yankees, they do it in moderation and with class.
>
> — *Michael Dean Jacobs, Dodgers fan*

> To a certain extent they do, however, a team like the Red Sox, for example, does not set the market price for players, the Yankees do. Yes, Boston and the Angels and Mets have more resources than do other teams; however, the Yankees are the 800 lb. gorilla here, and the other "large market teams" are merely trying to keep up with seventy percent of the resources the Yankees throw into the mix.
>
> — *Matt Kennedy*

That's the biggest lie in baseball. Every three to four years the Red Sox and Mets will pick up a perennial all-star/hall of famer, like Manny and Pedro [in 2000 and 2005, respectively]. The Yankees add four of those players every year. Let's just list the ones from the last six years that I can remember. Ahem, [deep inhale] Jason Giambi, Gary Sheffield, Kenny Lofton, Hideki Matsui, Alex Rodriguez, Randy Johnson, Mike Mussina, Kevin Brown, Carl Pavano, Roger Clemens, not to mention Jose Canseco, Darryl Strawberry, and David Justice in the late '90s. And let's not forget their latest *coup de grâce* of purchasing Johnny Damon at the eleventh hour. Some came via trades because other teams didn't want to pay them. Somehow I don't think the Trot Nixon's and Timmy Wakefield's measure up to that roster. We are definitely part of the problem. But we are at level two with the Mets, and the Dodgers. The Yankees are in a spending "league of their own."

— *Bill Burr*

The difference between the Yanks and everyone else is that the Yankees can afford to take chances on players that are high risk and not worry about the consequences.

— *AV, Mets fan*

And finally, we hear from Mark Janney, a New York Yankee fan who was classy enough to cast all discrepancies aside long enough to bestow upon us the invaluable advice on how to quell the hatred toward the Yankees and Mr. Steinbrenner.

You should blame your crappy management who can't keep up with the latest financial trends. Perhaps Mr. Steinbrenner should've bought your team back in 1973. Maybe then he could have shown you all how a real class franchise should be run.

The immutable question prevalent to the discussion is: Where do Yankee fans get off ridiculing other teams for having a high salary? How insane is the salary structure in baseball? Yankee fans will try to convince you that baseball should have a salary *floor* or minimum salary instead of a *cap*. Why should they be penalized for having an endless stream of money? Grouping teams together by 2005 payroll in approximately $30 million increments and increasing the range in the luxury tax area, we begin to see how many different leagues there are. Looking at it this way certainly takes away a Yankee fan's arguing chips. Yeah, we know the Red Sox are second with an exorbitant salary and the Mets also far exceed the majority of other teams, but if you are a Red Sox or Mets fan, let the Royals fan chastise you and your team for this glaring discrepancy. To hear it from a Yankee fan is just silly.

Look, we get it: your owner is richer and wealthier than most of us could ever hope to be. But why should George be penalized for his bottomless checkbook? He is still playing by the rules. Ah, now we've come to the crux of the problem.

Except for the fact that he's an insane megalomaniac with a penchant for baseball's equivalent of a hostile takeover, George's spending is not the only problem; a similar, if not greater, problem is the Yankee fans' delight in winning with the unfair advantage their team has. We went into detail before about how they get excited about things that are supposed to happen. You can't prevent them from cheering their team. But the problem stems from the root of a Yankee fan's soul—their brazen arrogance. They have to rub it in. And so begins one of the most contentious arguments between these fans and fans of other high-priced teams. Though it hasn't happened in a while, here's what you'll be facing if and when the Yankees achieve another World Series victory by far outspending all comers.

YANKEE FAN: Yay! We won the World Series again!

OTHER FAN: You were supposed to with a $208 million payroll.

YANKEE FAN: You're just jealous. That's twenty-seven, baby!!!!

OTHER FAN: If any other team was in the same salary hemisphere, we'd be upset that we lost, but it's expected.

YANKEE FAN: Typical [insert team name here] fan, always whining when you lose.

OTHER FAN: It's the equivalent of arm-wrestling an eight-year-old. You'd better win!

YANKEE FAN: Your team spent more than most every other team and they still didn't win!

OTHER FAN: No, they lost to a team with a much greater payroll!!!

YANKEE FAN: Na-na, twenty seven. Na-na twenty seven . . .

And this goes on and on and on until you're Toronto Blue Jay blue in the face . . .

At this point, prepare to be told that you're just a "sore loser" or that's whining about "sour grapes." (Isn't it weird how a sore winner that *knows* they've won unfairly always claims the loser is just expressing sour grapes?) Is it whining to point this discrepancy out? Clearly, if you call a spade a spade, you're not bitching because it isn't a club. Yankee fans only resort to this feeble attempt to keep from listening to your logic. They don't want you raining on their parade because for right now, they are actually proud of their team's "accomplishment."

It's tough to get anything through their skulls right now. If you can, steer clear of this dispute. Not because you'll lose, but rather, because it's grounded in opinion and subjectivity. You can fly around in circles spewing your precious pros and cons against the opposite and the only thing you'll come away with is a migraine, cottonmouth, and a scorching case of angina. (It's a sore throat, you pervs!)

A DECADE OF DECADENCE

The summer of 1994 manifested the eighth work stoppage in MLB history. The players walked on August 12 and the season was aborted one month later. Citing a deterioration of the financial situation throughout the league, baseball owners now demanded a salary cap. The players were reluctant to accept such an "unfair deal." Obvious financial losses aside, baseball statisticians were foaming at the mouth, as a few hallowed records were about to be broken when the strike was called.

- Tony Gwynn (Padres)—His .394 batting average found him challenging Ted Williams' forty-three-year-old record to break .400.
- Matt Williams (Giants) - His forty-three home runs were on pace to break Roger Maris' record of sixty-one, four years before Mark McGwire and Sammy Sosa's "performance-enhanced" run for the record.
- Even the subterranean-dwelling Montreal Expos led the NL East by six games.

Alas, there would be neither playoffs nor World Series that season. Fortunately for most of the baseball world, a strike really only affected the Yankees and their demanding fans. When baseball resumed on April 25, 1995, it crossed the threshold into the "modern playoff era." Eight teams would now enter the post season (the three division leaders and one wildcard team from each league . . . Oh, you know how it works . . .)

In keeping with our debate about "money buys championships," all our hard work climaxes on the following pages. We thought we'd provide some key stats compiled over the last ten years to help you decide for yourself. Note how quickly salaries have escalated. Which team seems to have led the way? Hmmm . . .

During each year, payroll fluctuations occur due to midseason acquisitions and other transactions. Some charts list annual salary with luxury tax additions, some state the opening day numbers, and some use the average number throughout the season. We found numbers that at some point during the season represent the amount each team spent on its players. Trust us on this one; the institute IS accurate . . . frequently.

= Wildcard team

1995

Team	Win	Loss	GB	Payroll	Rank	Year End Result
New York Yankees*	79	65	7	$58,165,252	1	Lost ALDS 2-3
Baltimore Orioles	71	73	15	$48,739,636	2	7th worst AL record
Cincinnati Reds	85	59	0	$47,739,109	3	Lost NLCS 0-4
Atlanta Braves	90	54	0	$47,023,444	4	Won WS 4-2
Toronto Blue Jays	56	88	30	$42,233,500	5	Worst record in MLB
Cleveland Indians	100	44	0	$40,180,750	6	Lost WS 2-4
Boston Red Sox	86	58	0	$38,157,750	8	Lost ALDS 0-3
Montreal Expos	66	78	24	$13,116,557	28	5th worst MLB record

In the first year after the strike, the Yanks again emerge as the team with the highest salary. Finishing second to Boston and earning the first ever AL Wild Card birth, they fail to make it out of the first round of playoffs (thank you, Seattle) as do the Sox. Three of the top five salaried teams went to the post season while the fourth and sixth ranked teams advanced to the Fall Classic. It's interesting to note that the Blue Jays, coming in at number five, finished with the worst record in baseball. Sorry folks, money helped, but ultimately bought nothing that year. Oh, but wait . . .

✦ ◇ ✦

1996

Team	Win	Loss	GB	Payroll	Rank	Year End Result
New York Yankees	92	70	0	$61,511,870	1	Won WS 4-2
Baltimore Orioles*	88	74	4	$55,127,855	2	Lost ALCS 1-4
Atlanta Braves	96	66	0	$53,797,000	3	Lost WS 2-4
Cleveland Indians	99	62	0	$47,686,907	4	Lost ALDS 1-3
Chicago White Sox	85	77	14.5	$44,827,833	5	Tied for 6th in AL
Boston Red Sox	85	77	7	$38,516,402	11	Tied for 6th in AL
Detroit Tigers	53	109	39	$17,955,500	26	Worst record in MLB
Milwaukee Brewers	80	82	19.5	$11,701,000	28	16th in MLB

The Yanks enter year one of their self-proclaimed "mini-dynasty." Four of the top five teams went to post while the top two money-ball clubs in each league squared off in the World Series. The poverty-stricken Brewers (thank you, Bud Selig) wallowed in mediocrity as the Tigers, with the third lowest payroll, held shut the basement door.

1997

Team	Win	Loss	GB	Payroll	Rank	Year End Result
New York Yankees*	96	66	2	$73,389,577	1	Lost ALDS 2-3
Baltimore Orioles	98	64	0	$64,611,399	2	Lost ALCS 2-4
Cleveland Indians	86	75	0	$58,865,056	3	Lost WS 3-4
Atlanta Braves	101	61	0	$53,111,000	4	Lost NLDS 2-3
Florida Marlins*	92	70	9	$52,465,000	5	Won WS 4-3
Boston Red Sox	78	84	20	$40,611,351	13	6th worst AL record
Oakland Athletics	65	97	25	$12,879,889	28	Worst record in MLB

We see the Yanks three-peat in payroll in the post-strike era. They again won the wildcard and again never made it through round one of the playoffs. Ha ha . . . however, for the first time, all five top money teams played in October. Meanwhile, the A's picked up wins in both lowest payroll and worst record. In Vegas, this year would've been considered a push.

1998

Team	Win	Loss	GB	Payroll	Rank	Year End Result
Baltimore Orioles	79	83	35	$74,170,921	1	7th worst AL record
New York Yankees	114	48	0	$73,963,698	2	Won WS 4-0
Texas Rangers	88	74	0	$62,755,368	3	Lost ALDS 0-3
Atlanta Braves	106	56	0	$61,840,254	4	Lost NLCS 2-4
Los Angeles Dodgers	83	79	15	$60,731,667	5	8th in NL
Boston Red Sox	92	70	22	$59,547,000	6	Lost ALDS 3-4
San Diego Padres	98	64	0	$53,081,166	10	Lost WS 0-4
Florida Marlins	54	108	52	$19,141,000	26	Worst record in MLB
Montreal Expos	65	97	41	$8,317,500	30	Does it really matter?

[NOTE:] *The Devil Rays & Diamondbacks expansion teams were added in 1998*

Okay Yankee fans, this is the moment you've been waiting for . . . a little vindication. This was the first year the Yankees won the World Series without the highest payroll. Oh, and how they use this ONE and ONLY time as ammunition to thwart accusations of "buying the crown." But they fail to mention that they were second only by a mere $207,223 (roughly the same amount they now pay A-Rod for 1.5 games) and $11.2 million more than the next closest team. Still, shame on the O's for sucking their way into deflating a perfectly good Yankee myth. Once again, the small salaried teams picked barnacles off the barge.

1999

Team	Win	Loss	GB	Payroll	Rank	Year End Result
New York Yankees	98	64	0	$91,990,955	1	Won WS 4-0
Texas Rangers	95	67	0	$80,801,598	2	Lost ALDS 0-3
Atlanta Braves	103	59	0	$79,256,599	3	Lost WS 0-4
Cleveland Indians	97	65	0	$73,531,692	4	Lost ALDS 2-3
Boston Red Sox	94	68	4	$72,330,656	5	Lost ALCS 1-4
Minnesota Twins	63	97	33	$15,845,000	29	Worst record in MLB
Florida Marlins	64	98	39	$14,650,000	30	2nd worst record in MLB

If ever there was a year that payroll all but guaranteed a spot in the post season, this was it. All five top money teams saw extended seasons. The top two teams in each league again took a limo to the prom while the penniless remained on Skid Row. Money did all the talkin' this year.

2000

Team	Win	Loss	GB	Payroll	Rank	Year End Result
New York Yankees	87	74	0	$92,538,260	1	Won WS 4-1
Los Angeles Dodgers	86	76	11	$88,124,286	2	5th best NL record
Atlanta Braves	95	67	0	$84,537,836	3	Lost NLDS 1-3
Baltimore Orioles	74	88	13.5	$81,447,435	4	4th worst AL record
Arizona D-backs	85	77	12	$81,027,333	5	7th in NL
New York Mets	94	68	1	$79,509,776	6	Lost WS 1-4
Boston Red Sox	85	77	2.5	$77,940,333	7	6th best AL record
Minnesota Twins	69	93	26	$16,519,500	30	2nd worst record in MLB

Indeed, an odd year money-wise. Only two of the top five teams advanced. But, as usual, the victor already has all the spoils. On a lighter note, this year marks the last championship win for the Yanks to date.

◆ ◇ ◆

2001

Team	Win	Loss	GB	Payroll	Rank	Year End Result
New York Yankees	95	65	0	$109,791,893	1	Lost WS 3-4
Boston Red Sox	82	79	13.5	$109,558,908	2	6th best AL record
Los Angeles Dodgers	86	76	6	$108,980,952	3	7th best NL record
New York Mets	82	80	6	$93,174,428	4	9th best NL record
Cleveland Indians	91	71	0	$91,974,979	5	Lost ALDS 2-3
Arizona D-Backs	92	70	—	$81,206,513	8	Won WS 4-3
Tampa Bay D-Rays	62	100	34	$54,798,500	13	Worst record in MLB
Minnesota Twins	85	77	6	$24,350,000	30	5th best record in AL

Again, only two of the top five teams moved on this year and only one of those played through the harvest moon. (Guess who?) The *homegrown* Twins, however, sporting by far the lowest payroll, finished with an impressive fifth best record in the AL. And although people tend to paint the storied D-Backs as the needy kids from the wrong side of the tracks who felled the gold-cloaked behemoths, they ranked eighth in payroll. Not too shabby. But at the end of the day, all that matters is that they dethroned the Money Kings and started a fad that is still popular around the league to this very day.

2002

Team	Win	Loss	GB	Payroll	Rank	Year End Result
New York Yankees	103	58	—	$125,928,583	1	Lost ALDS 1-3
Boston Red Sox	93	69	10.5	$108,366,060	2	5th best AL record
Texas Rangers	72	90	31	$105,302,124	3	5th worst AL record
Arizona D-backs	98	64	—	$102,820,000	4	Lost NLDS 0-3
Los Angeles Dodgers	92	70	6	$94,850,952	5	5th best NL record
Anaheim Angels*	99	63	4	$61,721,667	15	Won WS 4-3
Tampa Bay D-Rays	55	106	48	$34,380,000	30	Worst record in MLB

This year marked just the second time the wildcard team went on to win the WS, and they did it from the middle of the pack in terms of bankroll. They also accomplished this impressive feat with only two names: 1) Anaheim and 2) Angels. Ah, the salad days . . . But more importantly, they effortlessly eliminated Daddy Warbucks & Co. in round one. In the interim, the impoverished Devil Rays slugged it out with the Tigers in the Battle of Suck.

2003

Team	Win	Loss	GB	Payroll	Rank	Year End Result
New York Yankees	101	61	—	$152,749,814	1	Lost WS 2-4
New York Mets	66	95	34.5	$117,176,620	2	4th worst MLB record
Atlanta Braves	101	61	—	$106,243,667	3	Lost ALDS 2-3
Los Angeles Dodgers	85	77	15.5	$105,872,620	4	2nd in NL West
Boston Red Sox*	95	67	6	$99,946,500	6	Lost ALCS 3-4
Florida Marlins*	91	71	10	$49,050,000	24	Won WS 4-2
Detroit Tigers	43	119	47	$49,168,000	25	Worst record in MLB
Tampa Bay D-Rays	63	99	38	$19,630,000	30	2nd worst record in MLB

Money got its ass kicked by way of the wildcard Florida Marlins, who possessed one of the lowest salaries in the game. Bummer . . . On the under-card, the Tigers out-sucked their rivals from Tampa en route to claiming the second worst record in major league *history*. That illustrious honor goes to the 1899 Cleveland Spiders who finished the season with a 20-134 record. But honestly, who doesn't know that?

2004

Team	Win	Loss	GB	Payroll	Rank	Year End Result
New York Yankees	101	61	—	$182,835,513	1	Lost ALCS 3-4
Boston Red Sox*	98	64	3	$125,208,542	2	Won WS 4-0
Anaheim Angels	92	70	—	$101,084,667	3	Lost ALDS 3-0
New York Mets	71	91	25	$100,629,303	4	4th worst NL record
Philadelphia Phillies	86	76	10	$93,219,167	5	2nd in NL East
St. Louis Cardinals	105	57	—	$75,633,517	12	Lost WS 0-3
Arizona D-backs	51	111	42	$70,204,984	14	Worst record in MLB
Milwaukee Brewers	67	94	37.5	$27,518,500	30	4th worst record in MLB

Again, three of the five top teams advanced. It was also sad to see how far Arizona has fallen from grace in talent and payroll, (dropping $32.6 million over the previous two seasons). Their fans would've been quite disgraced if they had not melted during a home stand in August. Overall, this is an ideal example of how the dynamics of the game are directly related to the . . . wait a minute; the wildcard Red Sox won the World Series? Is that stat right?

2005

Team	Win	Loss	GB	Payroll	Rank	Year End Result
New York Yankees	95	67	—	$208,306,817	1	Lost ALDS 2-3
Boston Red Sox*	95	67	—	$125,208,542	2	Lost ALDS 0-3
New York Mets	83	79	7	$101,305,821	3	5th(t) in NL
Anaheim Angels	95	67	—	$97,725,322	4	Lost ALCS 1-4
Philadelphia Phillies	88	74	2	$95,522,000	5	2nd in NL East
Houston Astros*	89	73	11	$76,779,000	12	Lost WS 0-4
Chicago White Sox	99	63	—	$75,178,000	13	Won WS 4-0
Tampa Bay D-Rays	67	95	28	$29,363,067	30	2nd worst record in MLB

Yet another three-for-five year for the top money teams. And none of them made it to the grand stage. Those honors went to the middle of the pack twelfth and thirteenth ranked teams, with the 'stros taking the NL wildcard. Once again the Yankees' spending trend of distancing themselves from the pack continued (*unsuccessfully, we might add*). Let's review . . .

- The Yankees payroll was more than double that of every team except the Red Sox and in that case, it's a whopping seventy-five percent higher.
- The gap between the Yankees and the next highest team is equal to or greater than the entire payroll of all but ten teams.
- Take away the Yankees starting infield (including the market-raising salaries of Giambi, Jeter, and A-Rod) and they would still have a higher payroll than every other team.
- While they did make it to the post season for the eleventh straight year, they still didn't win the World Series. In fact, they've spent nearly $780 million dollars since their last WS victory, only to pack up and go fishing early . . .

So what, you ask, does all this mean? Well, for starters, it should be distinguished that, prior to the new "modern playoff era," the

Yankees had the highest payroll *every single* year they won the World Series. Unfortunately, as we mentioned, that legacy would expire in 1998, courtesy of "those damn Orioles." (*Someone should turn that travesty into a play. Perhaps Harry Frazee's grandson could even hawk some of Babe's old memorabilia to finance it.*) That being said, it's obvious the Yankees are able to protect themselves and ride out any storm a long season can muster. An All-Star starting pitcher goes down? No problem. Four All-Star starting pitchers go down? Just seamlessly slide a couple more in as stop gaps. Need to eliminate the competition? Prevent other teams from getting players by snatching them away.

Basic economics demonstrate that spending money without revenue will bankrupt you in no time. So how do you keep up with a money machine like the Yankees? Well, other teams have added more seats, food concourses, raised ticket prices, etc. yet they STILL can't touch the Yankees spending spree. We've evaluated hundreds of suggestions for a quick fix toward preventing further escalation of player salaries and team spending. It was Met fan Billy Abelson, who undeniably presented the ultimate proposal—"Decertify Scott Boras!"

The truth is; anything less than a Yankee victory is a monumental collapse. The very foundation Georgie has created not only allows All-Stars at every position, but also the replenishing safety net of same-caliber players should anything happen. Once you're the highest salaried team in the world, what difference should it make if you're $10 million more than the next highest or at a mark up of sixty-six percent or $80 million? If you're gonna make a mockery of the system, might as well go all the way, right? So they spend and spend and spend and spend . . .

Now, do the Yankees actually buy their championships? Since they don't have any in this century, the answer would be a resounding "no." But, rephrase the question and it makes an argument more feasible; money may not buy a World Series crown, but if you consistently spend anywhere between fifty percent and *seven hundred percent* more than any other team, it all but *guarantees* your club a seat at the playoff table, no questions asked. And there's where you can stuff a rosin bag in any Yankee fans' mouth— you know it'll be open!

Inarguably, it's a different game that the Yankees play and although it has some elements of the game of baseball, it isn't the twenty-nine other teams more rooted in the traditional national pastime play. Sure, the Yankees haven't won the World Series since the dawn of the millennium, but spending a great deal more than everybody else WILL inevitably pay off. They're merely playing the odds with "house money." Each year, they get better at that strategy of overpaying. Sometimes it doesn't work because of typical circumstances like a lack of team chemistry or a deluge of injuries, but EVENTUALLY the Hummer will run the Honda off the road.

Finally, in the interest of fairness and love of the game, we believe that the playing field, as it were, would be best served on a level surface. But why listen to us? This is about you, the amazing fans out there whose continual support of baseball (through viewership and attendance) actually pays these players salaries. You truly are a benevolent lot. You think with your hearts, not your wallets. That is why it is your voice that matters most.

That being said, wouldn't a second or third copy of this book make excellent gifts? Then, the authors would be well on their way to "Steinbrenner dough" and could afford ghostwriters so they'd never have to lift a finger or a brain cell again!

CHAPTER TWELVE—
TAKE THIS JOKE AND . . . SHOVE IT!

Up until now, you've absorbed a lot from the previous chapters in terms of the verbal tango with members of the evil empire fan base. Lest we give you the wrong idea, it doesn't always have to feel like you're walking on eggshells, aside from when they try to set your hat on fire with your head still in it. There are moments of levity too. Everyone loves a good joke. And as animosity can rise, defusing the tension with a chuckle is a good idea.

The *How to Talk to a Yankee Fan Institute* has compiled all those jokes for you, to be committed to memory for use when the mood is right. Wearing rainbow suspenders and having a squirting lapel flower is unnecessary to win people over with these gems. Feel free to pass these along to other friends as well for them to use on Yankee fans. We're sure you've heard some of these before, as they're very popular. Many are based on true stories . . . *(especially the last one about George!)*

Q: Did you hear that the Post Office just recalled their latest stamps?
A: They had pictures of Yankees players on them . . . people couldn't figure out which side to spit on.

Q: What do you have when 100 Yankee fans are buried up to their neck in sand?
A: Not enough sand.

Q: Why is it good to be driving with a Yankee fan?
A: You can park in the handicap zone!

Q: What's the difference between a dead dog and a dead Yankee fan lying in the road?
A: There are skid marks in front of the dog.

Q: You're trapped in a room with a tiger, a rattlesnake, and a Yankee fan. You have a gun with two bullets. What should you do?
A: Shoot the Yankee Fan . . . Twice!

Q: What's the difference between Bigfoot and a smart Yankee fan?
A: Big Foot has been sighted before!

Q: What do Yankee fans use for birth control?
A: Their personalities.

Q: What has 400 feet and three teeth?
A: The first row of the bleachers at Yankee Stadium.

Q: What do Yankee fans and sperm have in common?
A: One in 3,000,000 has a chance of becoming a human being.

Q: What's the biggest challenge for the Yankees marketing department?
A: Literacy!

Q: What does your average Yankee fan get on an IQ test?
A: Drool.

While on tour around America, the Pope was relaxing on a New England beach. He was looking out at the water and saw a man in a Yankee cap being attacked by a shark. The Pope initially panicked, but then saw two men in a boat, both wearing Red Sox caps, pull the man and the shark into the boat. When they came to the shore, the Pope approached the Sox fans and praised them for being so brave and humanitarian, and  how they'd be rewarded in heaven. The Pope knew of the Sox/Yanks rivalry and was proud of them for putting their emotions aside to do God's work. He then blessed them and left. One Sox fan turned to the other and said, "Whatever . . . so how's the bait holding up?"

(The obvious question is, does the Pope wear his hat at the beach? And what might the appropriate papal SPF be? Try discussing that with a Yankee fan.)

Four baseball fans—one from Philadelphia, another from Boston, a Mets fan, and a Yankee fan—are climbing a mountain. On the way up they argue about how loyal they are to their team and what each would do for them. As the climb progresses, the stakes increase. Upon reaching the top, the Mets fan shouts, "This is for the Mets," and hurls himself off the top.

Next the Philadelphian yells, "This is for the Phillies," and leaps off the mountain. Suddenly, the Red Sox fan yells, "This is for everyone!" and pushes the Yankee fan off.

A Braves fan used to amuse himself by scaring every Yankee fan he saw strutting down the street in the obnoxious NY pinstripe shirt.

He would swerve his van as if to hit them, and swerve back just barely missing them.

One day, while driving along, he saw a priest. He thought he would do a good deed, so he pulled over and asked the priest, "Where are you going, Father?"

"I'm going to give mass at St. Francis church, about two miles down the road," replied the priest.

"Climb in, Father. I'll give you a lift." The priest climbed into the passenger seat, and they continued down the road.

Suddenly, the driver saw a Yankee fan walking down the road, and he instinctively swerved as if to hit him. But, as usual, he swerved back into the road just in time. Even though he was certain that he had missed the guy, he still heard a loud THUD. Not understanding where the noise came from, he glanced in his mirrors but still didn't see anything. He then remembered the priest, and he turned to the priest and said, "Sorry, Father, I almost hit that Yankee fan."

"That's OK," replied the priest, "I got him with the door."

A Sox fan, a Cubs fan, and a Yankee fan were all in Saudi Arabia performing military duty for the U.S. Army. While off base, they were caught smuggling a case of booze. All of a sudden, Saudi police rushed in and arrested them. The mere possession of alcohol is a severe offense in Saudi Arabia, so for the terrible crime they were sentenced to death! Their lawyers were able to successfully appeal their sentence down to life imprisonment.

By a stroke of luck, a benevolent Sheik decided that they could be released after receiving just twenty lashes of the whip. As they were preparing for their punishment, the Sheik said, "It's my eighth wife's birthday today, and she has asked me to allow each one of you one wish before your whipping."

The Cubs fan was first in line (he drank the least). He thought for a while and said, "Please tie a pillow to my back." This was done, but the pillow only lasted ten lashes before the whip went through. The Cubs fan was carried away bleeding and crying.

The Yankee fan was up next (*he almost finished an entire fifth by himself*), and after watching the scene said, "OK please fix two pillows to my back." But even two pillows could only take fifteen lashes before the whip went through again, sending the Yankee fan crying like a baby.

The Red Sox fan was the last up (*given his allegiance, he finished off the crate*) but before he could say anything, the Sheik turned to him and said, "You support the greatest baseball team in the world and your supporters are the best and most loyal fans in all the world. For this you may have two wishes"

"Thanks, your most royal highness'" the Red Sox fan replied. "In recognition of your kindness, my first wish is that you give me not twenty, but *one hundred* lashes."

"Not only are you an honorable, powerful man, you are also very brave," said the Sheik. "If 100 lashes is what you desire, then so be it. And your second wish?"

To which the Sox fan replied . . . "If you will sir, please tie the Yankee fan to my back."

A first grade teacher explains to her class that she's a Yankee fan and asks her students to raise their hands if they were Yankee fans too. Not really knowing what a Yankee fan was, but wanting to be like their teacher, hands explode into the air. There is, however, one exception—a girl named Lucy who has not gone along with the crowd.

The teacher asks her why she has decided to be different. "Because I'm not a Yankee fan." "Then," asks the teacher, "What are you?" "Why I'm proud to be a Twins fan!" boasts the little girl. The teacher is a little perturbed now, her face slightly red. She asks Lucy why she is a Twins fan. "Well, my mom and dad are Twins fans, and I'm a Twins fan, too!"

The teacher is now angry. "That's no reason," she says loudly. "What if your mom was a moron, and your dad was a moron, what would you be then?" She paused, smiled and said, "Then, I'd be a Yankee fan."

Two boys are playing hockey on a pond in suburban Chicago when a rabid Rottweiler attacks one. Thinking quickly, the other takes his stick and wedges it down the dog's collar and twists, breaking the dog's neck. A reporter nearby sees the incident and rushes over to the boy. He starts writing in his notebook, "Young Cubs Fan Saves Best Friend From Vicious Animal,"

"But I'm not a Cubs fan," the little hero replied.

"Sorry, since we are in Chicago, I just assumed you were," said the reporter. "White Sox Fan Rescues Friend From Horrific Attack," he continued writing in his notebook.

"I'm not a White Sox fan either," the boy said. "I assumed everyone in Chicago was either for the Cubs or White Sox. Who do you root for?" the reporter asked.

"I'm a Yankee fan," the child replied. The reporter instantly scribbles in his notebook, "Little Bastard From New York Kills Beloved Family Pet."

Albert Einstein arrives at a party and introduces himself to the first person he sees and asks, "What is your IQ?" The man answers, "241." "That's wonderful!" says Albert. "We'll talk about the grand unification theory and the mysteries of the universe. We've much to discuss!"

Next, Albert introduces himself to a woman and asks, "What is your IQ?" She answers, "144." "That is great!" says Albert, "We can discuss politics and current affairs. We will have much to discuss!"

He approaches another person and asks, "What is your IQ?" The person answers, "Fifty-one." Albert ponders this for a moment, then smiles and says, "GO YANKEES"!!

A Baltimore fan, a Tampa Bay fan, and a New York Yankee fan are walking to the ballpark for a friendly spring training exhibition game when they see a body sticking out of some bushes. An inspection revealed a dead-drunk naked woman. The Oriole fan placed his cap on her right breast, the Devil Rays fan placed his cap on her left breast, and the Yankee fan put his over her crotch.

Then they called the police. The cop lifted up the O's cap and made a few notes. He then lifted the Devil Rays cap and made more notes. Then he lifted the Yankees cap, put it down, lifted it again and put it down. When he lifted it the third time, the Yankee fan said, "What are you doing? Are you some kind of pervert, or what?" The cop said, "I was just confused . . . usually when I see a Yankee cap, there's an asshole under it."

Two Yankee fans are on a train to watch a baseball game. They start making fun of a couple of Blue Jays fans that have only one ticket between both of them. Just before the conductor appears, both Jays fans slip into the bathroom, locking the door behind them. When the conductor knocks on the door, they slip the ticket under the door, he clips it, slides it back under, and off he goes.

On the return trip, the Yankee fans decide to pull the same trick and purchase only one ticket for both of them. They notice that, yet again, the two Jays fans have only one ticket between them. The Yankee fans realize there's only one bathroom per car and quickly take the lead, locking themselves in before the Jays fans—leaving them nowhere else to go. One minute later, the Jays fans without any tickets, stroll over to the bathroom and knock on the door . . .

Did you hear the one about Yankee Stadium falling apart? A huge beam fell through the deteriorating roof. In fact, this was the first time the Yankees have had a problem with crack without it resulting in the suspension of a player.

(We admit, that one's a little dated, as most of the Yankees haven't been doing crack since the '80s. However, it can easily be reworked to be more topical and mention steroids.)

Little Timmy was in his 4th grade class when the teacher asked the children what their fathers did for a living. All the typical answers arose; fireman, policeman, salesman, etc.

Timmy was being uncharacteristically quiet, so the teacher asked him about his father. "My dad is an exotic dancer in a gay cabaret and takes off all his clothes in front of other men. Sometimes, if the offer's really good, he'll go out to the alley with some guy and make love for money."

The teacher, obviously shaken by this statement, hurriedly set the other children to work on some coloring, and took little Timmy aside to ask him, "Is this really true about your father?"

"No," said Timmy, "He plays for the New York Yankees, but I was too embarrassed to say so."

POKIN' FUN AT GEORGIE

No joke book would be complete without some shots at "The Boss." (And we ain't talking about Bruce Springsteen.)

Q: How can you tell George Steinbrenner is lying?

A: His lips are moving.

The very day after George Steinbrenner's death, he called from Hell and vehemently challenged God to a baseball game. Smiling, God laughed, "You don't have a chance! I have Ruth, Mantle, and all the rest of the great Yankees up here!" "Yeah, so . . . " snickered George, "I have all the umpires."

George Steinbrenner walks into the doctor's office and says, "Doc, I've got an embarrassing problem. Now please, promise me you won't laugh!" "Of course I won't laugh," the doctor says. "I'm a professional. In twenty years, I've never laughed at a patient."

"Okay then," George says, proceeding to drop his trousers and revealing the tiniest penis, including infants, the doctor has ever seen. Unable to control himself, the doctor starts giggling, and then begins laughing uncontrollably. After a few minutes he manages to regain his composure enough to wipe the tears from his eyes.

"Sir, I'm so sorry," he says, "I really am . . . I don't know what came over me. On my honor as a doctor and a gentleman, I promise it won't happen again. Now, what seems to be the problem?"

"It's swollen."

There you have it, every last one of them. Be wary, Yankee fans may try to substitute your team in place of theirs in these jokes. Don't buy it. Politely laugh and then correct their pronouns. And if they begin to get belligerent, just ask, "How do you keep a Yankee fan in suspense?" Walk away before he can answer.

CHAPTER THIRTEEN—
THE MEANING OF LIFE

(Author's note: you didn't think we'd actually have a **Chapter Thirteen** in a baseball book, did you? We're much too superstitious for that.)

CHAPTER FOURTEEN—
DEYANKIFYING THE MASSES

"HELLO, MY NAME IS DAVE AND I'M A YANKEE FAN."

Over the last few decades, America has been engaged in a war on addictions ranging from drug abuse to compulsive gambling to overeating, and a host of other personal conflicts. There are two kinds of addiction—simple and complex. Psychologists have recently exposed the latest growing complex addiction that is plaguing millions of Americans, "Yankaholism."

Recuperation from "Yankaholism" is regarded as a tormenting process fraught with peril. The road to recovery can feel like a life sentence with no guarantee of success. If you or someone you know suffers from this addiction, there are programs out there that can help. To begin, you or the person you are concerned about should take this test below. You'll begin to realize that you are not alone. And the symptoms you thought were just personal "quirks" are actually indicative of a far greater crisis.

Y.A.—Yankaholics Anonymous

1. **Have you ever decided to stop rooting for the Yankees for a week or so, but it only lasted through the second inning?** *Most Y.A. members had told themselves secretly that they would want to choose another team, but never went through with it for fear of bringing shame to themselves, their friends, their family, and their family's friends. Here at Y.A., we teach you to take it slowly. Our credo is; "One inning at a time."*

2. **Do you wish people would just let you be and stop telling you how much you suck?** *At Y.A., we do not pass any judgments on you. We only share stories about how much we sucked, why we sucked, and*

all the suckey things we did as Yankee fans. We're happy to help you, but only if you want to be helped.

3. **Have you ever visited a library in the hopes that it would prevent you from yelling out insults to random people around you?** *We've all tried curbing our loud belligerence. We listen to Chopin while whittling blocks of wood into butterflies. We watch the Yankees' farm team with our church group. We avoid reading the sports pages or watching highlights. You name it; we tried it. But the instant any mention of the Yankees arises, something comes over us and we can't control ourselves, even during the reverend's Sunday sermon.*

4. **Have you ever had the shakes so bad; you needed to listen to a Mel Allen recording to get them to go away?** *If a physical problem can only be remedied by an exposure to anything Yankees, you most certainly have a problem. This is a sign that you are not a "passive" fan.*

5. **Do you envy people who actually like the sport of baseball and not just the Yankees?** *At one time or another, most of us have wondered why we can't just enjoy a game without mocking the other team or feeling that we have a sense of entitlement that everyone else is jealous of. Why are we not like other people who can just root for a spirited contest?*

6. **Has your Yankee allegiance caused trouble at home?** *Be honest! Doctors say that if you have a problem with rooting for the Yankees and continue to do so, it can only get worse—never better. Eventually, you'll be unable to deal with the reality that the Yankees are not going to win the World Series every year. You'll get all hunched up with a wrinkly face, looking to pick a fight (if you aren't like that already). The only hope is to stop rooting for the Yanks.*

7. **Do you ever stay at "the Stadium" after the cleaning crew is finished wondering when the next game is going to start?** *Most folks*

like to stay after a game for a few minutes to soak up the atmosphere. Yet after the ushers herded you out, do you ever find yourself hiding in the bathroom only to resurface later in a different section?

8. **Have you missed days of work or school because of misdemeanors caused when you threw something (or yourself) onto the field at Yankee Stadium?** *Many of us admit now that we "called in sick" lots of times when the truth was we exhibited a lack of judgment in self-control pertaining to our allegiance to the Yankees.*

9. **Do you tell yourself that you're not a rabid Yankee fan even as you get "Bernie Williams Forever" tattooed on your back?** *Many of us fool ourselves into thinking that we only root for the Yankees because our father did or because they are on TV all the time. After we came to Y.A., we saw that once we started rooting for the Yankees, we couldn't turn that part of us off.*

10. **Do you have pinstriped vision?** *Oy vay. The fact that you haven't sought professional help yet is frightening. If every object you see has stripes symmetrically aligned in a vertical pattern, you're in danger.*

11. **Have you ever felt that your life would be better if you were not a Yankee fan?** *Many of us became Yankees fan because it made life seem better, at least for a while. We were rooting for them to live and living to root for them. Here at Y.A. we now realize it is obvious that this is no way to live.*

12. **Have you ever awakened to realize that after last night's game, you killed a Red Sox or Mets fan?** *Y.A. might not be your first stop then. The police are looking for you. Though a Y.A. sponsor can be made available to visit you during the prison's visiting hours. This may be a great time to cure your addiction as Yankee gear and paraphernalia are not allowed on prison grounds, (because they have been found to incite riots).*

Did you answer **YES** to four or more of these questions? If so, you are in the "high-risk stage" of Yankee fandom. While Y.A. cannot guarantee to solve your life's problems, we can turn being a former Yankee fan from a "liability" into an "advantage." As a "born-again" fan you will start to enjoy the sport with renewed vigor. You can talk about subjects that pertain to everyone, like who's on "the juice" or which foreign pitcher escaped his native country to sign a big league deal for more than he's worth.

We'll show you that "one inning at a time" is more than just a mantra; it's a way of life. Without that first cheer, there can be no tenth and without that tenth, there can be no burning things and committing social injustices during celebration parades . . . if there are any. And if not, well, who cares? After all, baseball is only a game, right?

DEPROGRAMMING A YANKEE FAN

There is one more method available to make it bearable to be around Yankee fans, but it is quite extreme and very dangerous. The odds are not in your favor, though it has been done before. If the Yankee fan is acting his typical uncompromising (READ: dickish) self we suggest you try this ultimate act of recourse—deprogramming.

Deprogramming is a form of intervention to persuade a Yankee fan to leave his spurious cult and renounce all "programmed" beliefs. The world's top scientists and foremost authorities on deprogramming at the Bioinformatics Institute in Bern, Switzerland have found that less than one in one hundred Yankee fans will be converted in their lifetime. (*The actual number is .7 percent or seven in 1,000*)

Traditionally, candidates for deprogramming are innocent victims who've been subjected to mind control and brainwashing. Through this cerebral manipulation, their ability to think critically and to make independent decisions regarding baseball diamond discourse has been damaged by leaders who demand extreme loyalty, unquestioning faith, and do not tolerate open criticism of their ideas. David Koresh, Sun Myung Moon, George Steinbrenner, and L. Ron Hubbard are credited as the most notorious masters of this type of indoctrination.

The deprogramming process usually begins with abduction. The Yankee fan will have to be forced into a vehicle and taken on a daredevil ride to an isolated place somewhere in the Ozark Mountains. There, he is cut off from everyone but his captors who wear the uniforms of various teams in the league such as the Brewers, Astros, Tigers, and Royals. Members of the deprogramming group will then begin to bombard him with a multitude of questions, denunciations, and various schemes, all the while a rebroadcast of a Yankee game commentated by John Sterling is played in a continual loop. (Not even the most ardent devotee can stand John Sterling.)

Normally deprogramming only lasts a few days. In extreme cases the subject will be held against his will for months at a time until he recants his loyalty to the Yankees. When deprogramming a Yankee fan, you coerce them into something they've never done before: having an open mind and thinking rationally. The most essential part of "freeing the mind" is to convince the Yankee fan that he has unwittingly been held under control so he can see that "It is a gift to root for a championship team," "Other fans are not jealous of Yankee fans," "Buying your way into the playoffs is not fulfilling and is the emotional equivalent of beating a third-grader in arm wrestling," among other obvious facts. If successful, he'll realize he's been duped and his mind will start functioning properly.

Methods for Deprogramming

Isolation: The purpose here is to cut off Yankee fans from all interactions with the outside world. This includes denying them access to the YES Network, Sports Center, the *New York Post*, and any other possible media source so they won't be able to get updated scores, stats, and standings. Gradually, they'll begin to forget about their team and focus on their own survival. In extreme cases, the subject is confined to a "sensory depravation tank" until the desired results are achieved. The healing process begins when the subject snaps out of his self-induced trance and starts chanting things like, "Let's go, Cardinals!" and "Papi, Papi, Papi . . . "

Hypnosis: In the conventional hypnotic state, the Yankee fan will feel completely uninhibited, relaxed (expect some flatulence) and highly susceptible to the power of suggestion. This will also be characterized by heightened imagination and his fear of embarrassment will fly out the window. For example, if the hypnotist suggests that his tongue has swollen up to twice its size, the Yankee fan may suddenly feel panicky, start to sweat, and have trouble talking and, more importantly to his nature, spitting.

This is the perfect time for the hypnotist to implant the suggestive message. Example: "When I snap my fingers and say the word, 'Munson' you will wake up and forever be devoted to the Chicago Cubs because America loves an underdog. You will then renounce all allegiance the New York Yankees. You will despise them. In fact, every time you hear the words 'New York' or 'Yankees' in the same sentence, you will automatically begin a striptease while humming the theme song from *Petticoat Junction*.

Frontal Lobotomy: A surgery involving the severance of neural pathways in the brain's prefrontal lobe area to effect a change in behavior and correct severe mental illnesses such as; poor judgment, foul language, selective memory, motor function, and illicit sexual behavior. Today, lobotomies are practiced infrequently and are considered one of the last resorts for deprogramming intractable Yankee fans. Though as we discovered in Chapter One, it is almost impossible to work on a Yankee fan's brain without the use of a powerful electron microscope and tiny, tiny forceps.

Torture: Although considered by the Geneva Convention to be an extreme violation of human rights, the delegates decided to turn a blind eye to the infliction of severe physical or psychological pain for the extraction of information, confessions, and/or deprogramming a Yankee fan. Torture Methods include:

- Stretching Racks
- Electroshock Therapy
- Three-Beamed Harrows
- Juda's Cradle
- Head Presses
- Heretic Forks
- Rectal Pear
- Breast Talons (female only)
- Withholding Sex (male only)
- public humiliation by way of wearing extra large panties on their head with the NY logo sewn into the crotch area.

Exorcism: And if all other methods have failed, the final, sure-fire way to convert a Yankee fan is to perform the Catholic Rite of exorcism. This is the act of driving out demons and evil empire spirits from Yankee fans believed to be possessed by them. Signs of possession include; vomiting green Yankee Stadium dogs, speaking in strange tongue such as Aramaic, African Click, or Pig Latin, accompanied by cryptic messages like, "E. Pluribus Unum," "Domo arigato, Mr. Roboto," and "Papa was a Rolling Stone" appearing on the skin. Possessed Yankee fans will also, more often than not, repeatedly hit themselves in the crotch with a fungo bat.

The person performing the exorcism is often a priest or reformed ex-Yankee player such as Craig Nettles who are graced with special powers and skills. The exorcist uses a combination of prayers, hand gestures, amulets, and chalices filled with Holy water and Pete's Wicked Ale. The subject is also barraged with the incantation, "The Power of Ripken compels you!"

Often, when the spirits of evil empire have been vacated, the Yankee fan may experience stigmatic lesions shaped like Phil Rizzuto's head.

What to expect after deprogramming: The first few days back in society are critical for success. The "former" Yankee fan will sense a mellow calm inside and have more energy. However, they must prepare themselves for interactions with friends and family who'll try to lure them back, thus nullifying everything they've been through. They tempt them with the promise of "clean-cut, cuter players" and "more championships." Some may even offer their psychiatrist's number. Stay strong. Repeat the following mantra . . . "I will never turn to the dark side."

Side Effects: As with any medical or psychological procedure, there is always the chance for negative side effects. These may include any combination of the following:

- Migraine headaches
- Pin-striped vision
- Excessive fluid build-up in the mouth (from less spitting)
- A rash in the shape of the "NY" logo
- Singing "Sweet Caroline" out-of-the-blue
- Anal Leakage
- Reciting Yogi "Berra-isms" like, "Baseball is 90 percent mental. The other half is physical." And "Always go to other people's funerals; otherwise, they won't go to yours." And the classic "You better cut the pizza in four pieces because I'm not hungry enough to eat six."

Conclusion: As mentioned earlier, a full conversion can take anywhere from six days to a year as you need to record their reaction to the Yankees between March thru October . . . especially October! From time to time, in order to make certain that the deprogramming has been successful, it is recommended that the Yankee fan be hooked up to an EKG machine to monitor their brain waves and heart rhythms while they are shown pictures of Luis Gonzales, Jack McKeon, the 2002 champion Anaheim Angels and Curt Schilling's bloody sock.

In the event of withdrawal symptoms and a feeling to regress, watch *Field of Dreams* **immediately** to remind yourself that the sport of baseball is greater than any number of championships. And the next time you have a run-in with a Yankee fan, confidently look him dead in the eyes and say, "Hey . . . that really is an interesting butterfly . . . "

CONCLUSION

Well, there you have it . . . the groundwork has been laid and the ball is in their court now. You have the basic tools needed to coexist with our New York brethren using an open mind instead of a closed fist. (*Sure, they can be an uncultured, crass lot, but, unlike Raider fans, they're at least human.*) So let's forget the fists altogether and extend to them an olive branch of peace, restraining your desire to shove it up their [expletive + adjective + body part].

We suggest you be the bigger fan and expunge the years of torment at their hands. Even though they "can't handle the truth," (*A Few Good Men*) we ask you to "try real hard to be the shepherd here" (*Pulp Fiction*) and "Help me help you." (*Jerry Maguire*). Start anew. Open your heart to them. Don't show fear. They sense fear. Stand your ground and remember all we just taught you.

A few years ago, it may've been impossible to achieve this kind of détente, but heck, it also looked impossible for a team to blow a three-game lead in a League Championship Series. (Ooops, perhaps that isn't conducive to the detente we talked about so we request that it be stricken from the record . . . after you read it over a few dozen more times.)

And finally, because you've been such good students, we're going leave you with the final piece of this enigmatic puzzle. Many conspiracy theorists and prognosticators have died trying to obtain this priceless information. It's the ultimate cipher: a possession of knowledge as mysterious as Da Vinci's code or the identity of the second gunman. Sure, we could've told you this on page one, but what fun would that be? What would we have left to write about? So here it is, unveiled for the first time ever, the answer to the age-old question, "How can you to talk to a Yankee fan?" (Drum roll, please . . .)

You can't!!!

It's not from lack of trying, but you can't force them to be more civilized and agreeable. Just avoid them as much as possible, especially during baseball season . . . and the offseason.

Again, thank you for your purchase of *How to Talk to a Yankee Fan*.

APPENDIX I—
THE HTTTYF INSTITUTE 'S MAILBAG

The following are actual letters sent to us here at the *How to Talk to a Yankee Fan Institute*. After all, we are here to help you, the fan, any way we can!

Dear HTTTYF,
I'm attracted to this girl and want to ask her out, but just found out that she's a Yankee Fan. What should I do?
Brad, 24, Easton, PA

Dear Brad,
This isn't politics; this is *serious*. Go back and reread the section in Chapter Fourteen about deprogramming. If you still feel none of those options suit your needs, there are two other methods you may use to change her.
Method #1: Pay her off. Everyone has a price, and most Yankee fans are fickle when the greenbacks are involved. Some of them might even switch mid-game if the Yankees start to lose, or if something better comes along, or if it gets cloudy . . .
Method #2: Rent *50 First Dates* starring Adam Sandler and takes notes. Then, when no one is around, follow her home from work and run her car off the road into a tree. When she eventually wakes up, she'll have amnesia and won't even remember liking the Yankees in the first place. Be aware that you may run the risk that she'll completely forget who you even are. Oh, and it is also highly illegal. Joe Stebbins of New London, Connecticut accomplished

this feat most recently in 2002 and will be eligible for parole in time for spring training in 2010.

Dear HTTTYF,
My roommate is constantly keeping me up by yelling at the screen when he watches the YES network replay after midnight. What should I do?
Seth, Syracuse University, sophomore

Dear Seth,
Kill him. No one will miss him. If you're one of those religious nuts that believes murder is wrong, then go ahead and just club him over the skull with until he cries, "Jeter's a fag!"
(Just kidding. That was a test. If you passed, your roommate is still alive. If not, well, we're no longer liable for any harm you caused because of the disclaimer inherent in the phrase "just kidding.")

Dear HTTTYF,
I am a die-hard Rockies fan who really believes that the Yankees are baseball's equivalent of the gold standard. But, whenever I get into a conversation with their fans, I can't come up with a good argument against their logic. For instance, they claim other teams are just jealous because their general management doesn't follow the Yankees' aggressive approach to free agency. How can you argue with that?
Aaron K., Sales Executive, Smith Barney

Dear Aaron,

You're right. It is very hard to argue with a Yankee fan . . . especially when you ARE one. Had you not said you were a Rockies fan, we may have believed your question. A "diehard" Rockies fan to boot? Why not say you're Keyser Soze or the Easter Bunny? We see right through your ruse and the flaws in your logic. And you call yourself a "sales executive"? You'd be hard pressed to find anyone who will buy your line of bull.

Dear HTTTYF,

My husband is a Yankee fan and he's trying to raise our kids as such. He even brainwashes them by telling them that the Red Sox won the World Series in 2004 because the Yankees got tired of seeing them suffer. I love my husband dearly and he's a great father to our children, but I would rather he not plant these seeds of deception in their head. What should I do?

Kathy R., Sheffield, MA

Dear Kathy,

As with any disagreement in the tenuous arena of marriage, tact should be used. We suggest a romantic candlelight dinner and soft music where you can breach the subject over a carafe of his favorite Shiraz. Respectfully explain to him that you are uncomfortable with his "conspiracy theory" and how you wish you both could be on the same page when teaching the kids.

Treat him with tender passion throughout the evening. Enter your bedroom and make sweet love to him until the sparrows sing and the morning sun peaks over the horizon. Then, while he's sleeping blissfully in your arms, pour a small amount of chloroform onto a hand-kerchief and place it gingerly over his nose until he inhales the fumes. When you are absolutely certain that he's out cold, pack up the car, and take the kids to a remote place where you'll begin a new idyllic life under assumed names.

Dear HTTTYF,

One sticky subject in talking with those jerks is deter-mining if they've won a World Series in this century. We go back and forth arguing this and it's annoying the hell out of me. What say you?

Heidi Meadows, Boynton Beach, FL

Dear Heidi,

Well, if we imagine that the first century runs from the moment Jesus (the real one, not Johnny Damon) was killed, then we're talking about the year one. [It would read "January 1, 1" in your checkbook.] It runs until the year 100. Then the second century would logically begin at midnight on January 1, 101. This holds to form until the twenty-first century that began on January 1, 2001. The Yankees last won a championship in 2000, which was way back in the nineteenth century.

If, however, you are of the reasoning that Year One was actually Year Zero *until* Year One as in "January 1, 0" and the century ended at 11:59 p.m. on December 31, 99, then you are most definitely a Yankee fan grasping at straws with only a fleeting knowledge of the Roman calendar.

Dear HTTTYF,

Recently, I attended an interleague game at Yankee Stadium dressed in my Padres colors. Early in the game I was verbally abused by two children around seven years of age. They used words I had never heard before in my fifty-nine years; and I'm a former naval officer! I assumed the parents would reprimand the youths but on the contrary, they were egging them on. I plan to return to Yankee Stadium later this summer. If this happens again, how should I react?

Admiral Dean Redding, Ret., Padre fan

Dear Admiral,

Well, you must remember that "boys will be boys" and they are merely children engaging in typically harmless juvenile shenanigans. Any action against them, especially with the parents watching would be reprehensible. Therefore we recommend that you gut their parents with a crude prison shank. Once their parents are out of the way, you'll have those little orphan brats eating out of the palm of your hand. And ya know what? Screw 'em! (*Not literally*)

Dear HTTTYF,

I'm a Yankee Fan and I gotta say I don't like your book at all. You a-holes are just spreading hate! Yankee Fans aren't

bad people at all. You obviously haven't been to a game in Philly or Boston or Chicago. Those fans suck! Why not pick on them instead, ya piece of [expletive deleted]?
Yankeesrule26, the Bronx, NY

Dear Yankeesrule26,
We appreciate you making this book very easy for us.

APPENDIX II–
PRACTICE EXAM

Now it's time to put your schooling to the test and see what you've learned. These ten questions have been designed by the Scholastic Academy of Fundamental Discourse at the *HTTYF* Institute as a way to see if you are equipped to conversing with a Yankee Fan. There are no trick questions. Everything in the exam has been covered in the book. Just think carefully before you answer. Good luck!

I. **Math**: $a^2 + b^2 = c^2$ is an example of what theorem?
   a. Yogi Berra's
   b. The "Yankees have twenty-six championships" theorem.
   c. Something out of T.W.I.B. notes
   d. That moron who dove into the net behind home plate at Yankee Stadium.
   e. Pythagorean

The correct answer is (b). Remember we're dealing with a very limited number system here. The fact that you even considered a name instead of some sort of number commemorating Yankee greatness is appalling.

II. **Verbal**:
   Analogy - Yankee Stadium: _____:: apples:_____
   a. Yo' momma:: Yo' momma
   b. Camden Yards:: oranges
   c. The house that Ruth built:: the fruit that Ruth used in his martinis
   d. a suckier stadium:: a suckier fruit
   e. Yankee Stadium:: apples

The correct answer is (d). C'mon, you don't expect a Yankee Fan to acknowledge that there is a Stadium on earth as great as their own. And if you make the argument that the answer is (e), you'd have a good case based on the fact that many Yankee Fans don't know what an analogy is, and since they don't know what any of the answers mean, they would use this opportunity to use the word "suckier."

III. <u>Grammar</u>

(Change the underlined part to make it grammatically correct)

<u>Joe Torre, the manager of the Yankees,</u> has a tough choice to make in selecting his Opening Day starter.

a. Joe Torre, the Yankees' manager,
b. Yankee manager Joe Torre
c. Joe Torre, the greatest baseball manager to ever live and a hero to Italian-Americans everywhere,
d. Joe Torre, with four championship rings on his fingers,
e. Either a or b.

Any of these answers are grammatically correct, but only one succumbs to the rules of "Yankee Fan grammar." (C) not only puts him in his "rightful" place in the Pantheon of baseball greats using superlatives and hyperbole deftly, but it also exaggerates his worth to an entire population outside of the sport community. It's a two-for-one statement.

IV. <u>Reading comprehension</u>

I was at Fenway Park watching those Red Sux play my beloved Yankees the other day. (1) God, that place is a dump! It should be burned down and turned into a parking lot . . . with all those morons still inside at the time. They're nothing but a bunch of thugs there. I even saw a fight break out. You'd never see that at Yankee Stadium. (2) The fans are too dignified there.

During the game, I saw proof that the league is against the Yankees. A fan reached out and grabbed an easy fly ball out away from whoever the Yankees centerfielder was today and the batter was awarded a home run. (3) Geez, the Yankees never get calls like that. The Commissioner obviously wanted Boston to win. That's why he allowed the Red Sox to get Schilling even though Schilling wanted to go to the Yankees.

(4) The Yankees would have fifty championships if the rules weren't stacked against them. Especially with Joe Torre at the helm. He's never the manager of the year cuz it would kill the baseball writers to give it to a Yankee.

God, that park is making me sick. The seats face in the wrong direction, everything is so damn expensive, and that accent they all have! When are they gonna learn how to speak freakin' English?

1. It is clear from the first paragraph that the writer believes:
   a. he's right and everyone around him is wrong
   b. he is a fan of baseball on the whole
   c. the moon landing was staged in a Hollywood studio
   d. women owe him sex if he buys them a drink in a bar
   e. the Yankees need to add a seventh All-Star starting pitcher to their rotation

   (A) is the only answer. You're not going to be able to convince him of anything other than what he believes. Given his statements, you have to wonder if he's even been to Yankee Stadium.

2. Point (3) is an example of:
   a. an inflammatory statement
   b. glorified delusions
   c. trying to push your buttons
   d. a stable and idyllic family life
   e. all of the above

Although inflammatory statements are in his nature, the answer is (b). If he were trying to push your buttons, he would have to be conscious of the fact that what he's saying is both stupid and annoying to you. The fact that he lives in a world where the ocean is orange and beer falls from the sky on rainy days indicates he thinks he makes a lot of sense.

3. What does the author like to do in his spare time?
   a. Travel to Crazytown.
   b. Study accurate statistics based on diligent research
   c. Engage in spirited discussions
   d. Drink mass quantities of alcohol
   e. Root root root for the home team

Look no further than (a). Yes, he drinks heavily and when he speaks, he does so with spirit and passion, but he's had a summer home in the Wacko District ever since he saw his first pinstripe.

4. This can best be summarized as an essay about:
   a. the merits of friendly competition and fair play
   b. Don Henley's classic hit "The Boys of Summer"
   c. the socioeconomic connection between the rise in oil prices to the price of a 16 oz. beer
   d. a close-minded twit trying to spread his lunacy
   e. which sunscreen to use on a hot day

If you had been paying any attention at all, you'd know the answer is (e). His opinion on his recent baseball experience was unsolicited. The topic at hand was about sunscreen. The very mention of that word "sunscreen" reminded our subject about being in the sun at Fenway Park. He deemed the question irrelevant but his rant necessary.

V. **Multiple choice**: If the Yankees lose, you should start a conversation with . . .
   a. "Ha ha! The Yankees lost! They suck!"

b. "Don't worry, you still have twenty-six championships."

c. "That was bull****! The Yankees were robbed!"

d. "I hope you languish in hell, you maggot-infested pus bucket!"

e. Why would you actively seek out a conversation with a NY fan, especially when they're already bitter?

The answer, obviously, is (e). You can't win with any of the other options. (A) opens you up to a barrage of rhetoric pertaining to your team's incompetence compared to the entire history of the Yankees. (B) sounds like you're pandering and sympathetic. (C) makes it look as if you're being sarcastic. And (D), although accurate, is just begging for trouble.

VI. Say the Yankees are in a slump, should you rub it in?

a. without a doubt

b. only if the Yankee fan is bleeding from an orifice

c. yes, but in a passive-aggressive manner, like by accidentally replacing your live television feed with a loop of ESPN dissecting the slump and then having your friend over to "watch the game"

d. if the slump has kept the Yankees out of the playoffs, but stop before they can say "twenty-six championships"

e. never. It is undignified

You might be able to get away with (d), but only until they project their inner sorrow onto you and your "pathetic excuse for a ball club that'll take decades to even merit consideration being in the same league as the Yankees." Go with (c) as it leaves you more opportunity to feign ignorance as to your slow torture of him.

VII. **Yankee Traps** - You have a solid argument, but no facts to back it up, should you proceed forward?

a. Yes, you'll be able to make your point through circumstantial evidence.

b. No, a Yankee fan deserves to have all the facts laid out.

c. What difference does it make? You could wheel Thurman Munson's corpse up to Yankee fans and they'd still swear the catcher could call a better game than Carlton Fisk.

d. Yes, it's the makings of an intelligent back-and-forth

e. No, you couldn't possibly know what you're talking about if you have no iron-clad proof

The answer is easy. Even with proof, a Yankee fan is never found wrong, mainly because they deem the grounds for losing an argument is either admitting they lost, which they would never do, or having an umpire get bribed by the other team or commanded by the Commissioner to rule against them. Therefore, the answer is (c).

XI. **Essay**—Write an essay incorporating the following phrases:
- Twenty-six championships
- Don Mattingly is a definite Hall of Famer
- The Mets suck
- Greatest team in sports history
- Classy Yankee Fans

Okay, time's up. Please put your pencils down and hand your papers to the front of the class. It's time to grade your test results.

YOUR SCORE

1–3 correct = never get within 500 yards of a Yankee fan.

4–5 correct = don't make eye contact when around a Yankee fan

6–8 correct = just nod and smile when a Yankee fan talks to you

9–10 correct = Are you sure YOU'RE not a Yankee fan?

(As for the essay, we would grade you on them, but if you did a good job and actually incorporated all of those phrases, it would make us physically ill so just toss your work in the trash.)